What is Online Research?

'What is?' Research Methods series

Edited by Graham Crow, University of Southampton
ISSN: 2048–6812

The 'What is?' series provides authoritative introductions to a range of research methods which are at the forefront of developments in the social sciences. Each volume sets out the key elements of the particular method and features examples of its application, drawing on a consistent structure across the whole series. Written in an accessible style by leading experts in the field, this series is an innovative pedagogical and research resource.

What is Online Research?
Tristram Hooley, John Marriott and Jane Wellens

What is Social Network Analysis?
John Scott

What is Qualitative Research?
Martyn Hammersley

What is Discourse Analysis?
Stephanie Taylor

What are Qualitative Research Ethics?
Rose Wiles

What are Community Studies?
Graham Crow

Forthcoming books:

What is Qualitative Interviewing?
Rosalind Edwards and Janet Holland

What is Narrative Research?
Molly Andrews, Mark Davis, Cigdem Esin, Lar-Christer Hyden, Margareta Hyden, Corinne Squire and Barbara Harrison

What is Inclusive Research?
Melanie Nind

What is
online research?

Using the Internet for Social Science Research

Tristram Hooley
John Marriott
Jane Wellens

BLOOMSBURY ACADEMIC

First published in 2012 by

Bloomsbury Academic

An imprint of Bloomsbury Publishing Plc
50 Bedford Square, London WC1B 3DP, UK
and
175 Fifth Avenue, New York, NY 10010, USA

CIP records for this book are available from the
British Library and the Library of Congress.

ISBN 978-1-78093-334-4 (hardback)
ISBN 978-1-84966-524-7 (paperback)
ISBN 978-1-84966-555-1 (ebook)

This book is produced using paper that is made from wood grown in managed,
sustainable forests. It is natural, renewable and recyclable. The logging and
manufacturing processes conform to the environmental regulations
of the country of origin.

Printed and bound in Great Britain by the MPG Books Group, Bodmin, Cornwall

Cover design: Burge Agency

www.bloomsburyacademic.com

Contents

Contents

Series foreword

The idea behind this series is a simple one: to provide concise and accessible overviews of a range of frequently-used research methods and of current issues in research methodology. Books in the series have been written by experts in their fields with a brief to write about their subject for a broad audience who are assumed to be interested but not necessarily to have any prior knowledge. The series is a natural development of presentations made in the 'What is?' strand at Economic and Social Research Council Research Methods Festivals which have proved popular both at the Festivals themselves and subsequently as a resource on the website of the ESRC National Centre for Research Methods.

Methodological innovation is the order of the day, and the 'What is?' format allows researchers who are new to a field to gain an insight into its key features, while also providing a useful update on recent developments for people who have had some prior acquaintance with it. All readers should find it helpful to be taken through the discussion of key terms, the history of how the method or methodological issue has developed, and the assessment of the strengths and possible weaknesses of the approach through analysis of illustrative examples.

It is particularly appropriate for the first book in the series to be devoted to online research methods because they highlight methodological innovation's capacity to transform what we know about the social world. There is no better contemporary example of the point that as the social world changes, so must our research methods.

The books cannot provide information about their subject matter down to a fine level of detail, but they will equip readers with a powerful sense of reasons why it deserves to be taken seriously and, it is hoped, with the enthusiasm to put that knowledge into practice.

Graham Crow
Series editor

Acknowledgements

Thanks to Claire Madge and Henrietta O'Connor for inducting us into the world of online research methods, and to Rob Shaw and Julia Meek for exploring such methods with us.

Thanks to Graham Crow and Emily Salz for their patience and advice during the development of this book.

Thanks to Alan Cann and Tony Hirsh for a range of (online) conversations that informed the thinking in chapter 8.

Thanks to all at the International Centre for Guidance Studies, and to our families for bearing with us whilst this book was born.

Thanks to Korin Grant for sterling work proof reading the book.

1 Introduction

In 1999, Beaudouin and Velkovska introduced 'the Cyberians' to the academic world (Beaudouin and Velkovska 1999). These were not, as they may initially sound, some terrifying Dr Who monsters designed to send researchers rushing behind the sofa, but were actually members of an online community made up of users of a French internet service provider. Beaudouin and Velkovska analysed over 5000 messages posted on message boards, looked at the way individuals presented themselves on their homepages, interviewed eight of the Cyberians and received survey responses from an additional forty-two. Their main questions were essentially these – was it possible to describe the Cyberians as a community and, if so, what kind of community could exist made up of people who might never speak, touch, make eye-contact or meet?

Beaudouin and Velkovska concluded that the Cyberians did form a new kind of virtual community, but they also noted that the 'study raises more questions than it provides answers' (Beaudouin and Velkovska 1999: 8), and concluded that a whole new raft of research would be needed to understand this 'quickly expanding new social universe' (Beaudouin and Velkovska 1999: 9). They were not the first social researchers to investigate the internet, or to use online research methods for that investigation, but re-reading their study thirteen years later serves as a reminder of how quickly technology and social responses to technology move on. The online experience of community, which Beaudouin and Velkovska find in Cyberia, has now become a commonplace reality for millions, possibly even billions, of web users across the world. Through email lists, discussion boards and increasingly through social media such as Facebook and Twitter, social life and social interaction is something that happens online as much, or more, than it happens face-to-face.

The current generation of internet users are connected through social tools, and access online spaces through phones, televisions and gaming consoles as well as laptops and desktop computers. This generation would probably not describe themselves as belonging to online communities or see themselves as neo-Cyberians. Rather, they would see their online interactions as part of a wider, more inclusive, sense of the social. For most people Facebook does not foster the creation of an alternative online community, but rather supports the building and maintenance of face-to-face relationships (Ellison, Steinfield and Lampe 2007; Madge, Meek, Wellens and Hooley 2009; Burke, Kraut and Marlow 2011). Shirky summarizes this change, saying

> the old view of online as a separate space, cyberspace, apart from the real world, was an accident of history. Back when the online population was tiny, most of the people you knew in your daily life weren't part of that population. Now that computers and increasingly computer-like phones have been broadly adopted, the whole notion of cyberspace is fading. Our social media tools aren't an alternative to real life, they are part of it. (Shirky 2010: 537.)

Online research methods have been developed quickly and in response to rapid social and technological changes. The social world is being fundamentally reshaped, and it has been necessary for social research methods to respond to this change. As chapter 2 argues, the technologies which online research methods use are new in themselves, and the methodologies are even newer. Furthermore, as new technologies are created, social researchers have viewed them hungrily and sought to re-purpose them to the task of finding out about and understanding the social world.

This book, however, rejects the idea that the technology begets the methodology in any simple and straightforward way, and seeks to detail the inter-relationships between technologies, social forms and the methodologies that researchers use to investigate them. So the methodologies that a researcher might use to investigate something like the social gaming environment World of Warcraft (WoW) are shaped in response to the technology (what WoW allows users to do, what data it facilitates), and the social aspects of playing the game (why people play WoW and what kind of interactions they have). However, online research methods are also shaped by the rich methodological traditions that online researchers have to draw on. All of this talk of newness should not be allowed to obscure the fact that online research methods build on existing onsite research methods. Because of this, the core of this book has been organized around four chapters which detail how different methodologies are translated and reframed for the online environment: surveys in chapter 4; interviews and focus groups in chapter 5; ethnographies in chapter 6; experiments in chapter 7.

Online research methodologies therefore describe the approaches that researchers take, rather than the tools that they use. As this book will show, there has been a methodological conversation about online social research that has emerged out of wider methodological discussions. It begins from the question of how do researchers find out about and make sense of the social world, and particularly pursues that question in the context of the online environment. Online research methods do not describe an approach to finding out about the internet, but rather they describe an approach to finding out about people and the social world they inhabit, using the internet. Obviously along the course of that journey much is likely to be discovered about the technologies people use and how they use them, but that does not need to be the aim of every study that uses online research methods.

One of the biggest challenges that online researchers face is negotiating the ethical and legal complexity of the internet, and the new social formations that accompany it. As O'Hara and Shadbolt have argued, the culture of self-disclosure online has combined with increases in computing power to reshape what is understood by personal privacy (O'Hara and Shadbolt 2008). Legal and ethical frameworks are still struggling to catch up with these challenges, and the social researcher is at times left with little clear guidance. What is private and what is public is no longer clear, nor is it clear who has the legal right to give consent for the use of personal data in a world where proprietary software companies own enormous repositories of individuals' personal data. Add onto this that much online activity exists under multi-jurisdictional regulation, and that most states struggle to enforce regulations in relation to the internet. The online researcher is clearly in a challenging position, which is unlikely to be resolved through reference to a guidance booklet. Chapter 3 addresses these issues in more detail, and attempts to chart a pathway through them.

The audience for this book has been imagined as computer literate (but not techie) researchers with some experience of undertaking research in a face-to-face environment, but little or no experience of researching online. Because the book discusses a wide range of methodological traditions, and explores how they have been translated into online methods, each of the chapters is aimed at a non-specialist audience. While it does not attempt to provide a basic grounding in social science research, sugges-tions will be made of texts that can provide this grounding in each of the areas. This book also provides a glossary, to assist with the technological terminology that the online researcher is required to master.

One of the biggest challenges in working with online research meth-ods is that none of the methods has developed within disciplinary silos. Researchers in education, sociology, geography, psychology, economics and many other disciplines have been re-conceptualizing their approaches, and have been exploring how their methodological paradigms are reshaped by the use of online tools. In many cases this has led to creative inter-disciplinary cross-fertilization; however, this eclecticism can make the literatures difficult to access. Furthermore, it can present those attempting to synthesize the literature with an additional challenge of negotiating different epistemologies. This book reflects this inter-disciplinarity, and draws on a broad review of literatures in relevant disciplines without trying to resolve difference or privilege any particular approach. It does not claim to be a comprehensive literature review, but rather to provide an introductory text that is strongly grounded in published academic work.

There are lots of other excellent books that deal with the subject of online research methods. Many of them are discussed in chapter 2 and elsewhere throughout this book. However, as chapter 2 argues, relatively few books have as broad a focus as this volume. There are notable excep-tions to this, and it is useful to draw the reader's attention to Hine, Fielding *et al.*, Hesse-Biber and Leavy, and Gaiser and Schreiner, as particularly useful and comprehensive sources (Hine 2005; Fielding, Lee and Blank 2008; Hesse-Biber and Leavy 2008; Gaiser and Schreiner 2009). However, the speed of change in online technologies and methods means that there is considerable value in revisiting these issues regularly to explore how changes have reshaped methodological practices. This book therefore provides an up-to-date, comprehensive, multi-disciplinary work that maps the whole field of online research methods within the context of a rapidly changing technological landscape.

It is also important to note that online research methods cover a far wider set of approaches and strategies than the current volume can hope to address. For example, while the subject of online content analysis is touched on in chapter 6, it is not possible to do justice to it here. Other areas like online Delphi (Avery, Savelyich, Sheikh, Cantrill, Morris, Fernando, Bainbridge, Horsfield and Teasdale 2005) or usability and ergonomics (Rodriguez and Resnick 2010) are passed over altogether. However, in chapter 8 an attempt is made to look at 'where next for online research methods', and to deal with some of the more recent or more challenging areas of online research.

The book is designed to be read as a whole, although it is recognized that many people will dip into particular chapters as they embark on a particular project. However, while online research methods have to be understood as multi-faceted, there are challenges that are faced by all methodological approaches online. Because of this there is a considerable amount of cross-referral between chapters, and the online researcher will gain something by exploring the lessons that have been learnt in different methodological traditions.

It is hoped that this volume can provide new online researchers with insights about how to go about undertaking online research. It aims to offer practical solutions, without pretending that there is a one-size-fits-all approach to online research. It is also hoped that it can play a role in the cross-fertilization of ideas across different disciplines and methodological traditions. In a world populated by Cyberians, it is possible to argue that online research methods are too important to ignore.

Further reading

There is a wealth of good writing about current development in technology and the internet. Good starting points include *Here Comes Everybody* (Shirky 2009), which deals with the social and political implications of social media; *Everything Is Miscellaneous* (Weinberger 2008), which discusses the nature of information and authority online; *The Spy in The Coffee Machine* (O'Hara and Shadbolt 2008), which discusses the issue of privacy.

There are also a number of other introductions to the area of online research methods. *The Internet Research Handbook* (O'Dochartaigh 2001); *Internet Research Methods* (Hewson, Yule, Laurent and Vogel 2002) and *Online Research Essentials* (Russell and Purcell 2009) all offer good places to get started.

2 A brief history of online research methods

Online research has developed rapidly. Internet technologies are themselves relatively new, and their social impacts newer still. The theories and methodologies of online research have therefore developed in a technological and social environment that has changed year-on-year. This chapter will trace the interweaving of online research methods with this changing technological environment. It will reflect upon how methodological approaches and technologies have interacted, and how these interactions have created tensions and an imperative for continual methodological innovation.

All social research methods develop in relation to social, political and intellectual factors. How researchers approach their investigations is clearly intertwined with the world in which they live, and the subjects and themes that they are investigating. Various writers have traced the history of social research methods, including Platt and Alastalo (Platt 1996; Alastalo 2008). However, the latter argues that a comprehensive history of social research methods has still yet to be written because of the fragmented and multidisciplinary nature of what is being studied. In the absence of a definitive history, writers have tended to focus on a particular method or group of methods, such as qualitative approaches (Vidich and Lyman 1994; Platt 2002; Seale 2004), quantitative approaches (de Landsheere 1997; Tonkiss 2004; Cresswell 2005) and mixed method approaches (Tashakkori and Teddlie 1998; Cresswell 2003). Historical methodological reviews tend to argue that there has been a gradual increase in the pace of methodological development, but recognize that research methods are socially constructed and contingent on context. However, none of these historical methodological reviews contains much consideration of the development of online research methods, although many recognize that it is likely to transform research methods in the future.

This chapter addresses this omission in the historical literature by examining how technological changes, and in particular those associated with the growth of the internet, have impacted on the development of methodological thinking and practice. It is useful to begin with a timeline setting out key developments, in both the development of the internet and online research methods.

Table 2.1 Historical timeline

	Developments in internet technologies	Developments in online social research methods
1960s	Development of early forms of computer-mediated communication. 1962: Licklider sets out a vision for a 'Galactic' or 'Global' 'Information Network'.	
1970s	1973: first mobile phone demonstrated (Dr Martin Cooper of Motorola). 1979: first commercially automated cellular network (Tokyo, Japan).	
1980s	1983: first commercial handheld (not linked to a car) mobile phone (the DynaTAC 8000x). 1989: demonstration of the World Wide Web by Tim Berners-Lee.	1986: Kiesler and Sproull undertake an online survey (Kiesler and Sproull 1986). Invention of first computer packages for the analysis of qualitative data.
1990–1994	1990: public release of the World Wide Web. 1990: first search tool for the web (Archie) was created. 1993: first web crawler (Wanderer) was created. 1993: first graphical browser (Mosaic). 1994: Netscape browser launched. 1994: development of first popular search engines (Alta Vista, Lycos, Excite and Yahoo).	1993: Rheingold uses the term 'cyberspace'. 1994: Foster conducts online asynchronous interview using email. 1994: first methodological discussion of online interviewing (Brotherson 1994). 1995: *Journal of Computer-Mediated Communication* began publication.

	Developments in internet technologies	Developments in online social research methods
1995–1999	1995: Internet Explorer launched. 1995: first public video-conference took place. 1996: instant messaging services launched. 1997: Google released 1997: first weblog (blog) is attributed to Jorn Barger's Robot Wisdom Web site. 1997: SixDegrees.com is launched. Often seen as the first social networking site.	1995: Correll writes about 'internet ethnographies'. 1995: first online web experiment conducted. 1995: first comprehensive list of online psychological experiments published on the web. 1996: explosion of debate around online research ethics with papers published by Allen, Boehlefeld, King, Reid and Thomas (Allen 1996; Boehlefeld 1996; King 1996; Reid 1996; Thomas 1996). 1997: Krantz *et al.* publish an online psychology experiment in an academic journal (Krantz, Ballard and Scher 1997). 1997: World Wide Web and Contemporary Cultural Theory conference took place at Drake University.
2000–2004	2000: 400 million people across the globe use the internet. 2001: first commercial launch of 3G (Third Generation) mobile phones. 2001: first Access Grid developed at the University of Manchester. 2003: Myspace launched. 2004: development of Voice Over Internet Protocol (VOIP) telephone service. 2004: Mozilla Firefox web browser released (the 2nd most popular current browser after Internet Explorer). 2004: O'Reilly uses the term 'web 2.0'. 2004: Facebook launched.	2000: launch of the Association of Internet Researchers. 2000: publication of a number of key texts in the field, for example, *Mail and Internet Surveys. The Tailored Design Method* (Dillman 2000); *Virtual Ethnography* (Hine 2000); *Internet communication and qualitative research: A handbook for researching online* (Mann and Stewart 2000). 2001: *The Internet Research Handbook* published (O'Dochartaigh 2001). 2002: publication of *Online Social Sciences* (Batinic, Reips and Bosnjak 2002); *Internet Research Methods*, Hewson, Yule, Laurent and Vogel 2003); *Standards for internet-Based Experimenting* (Reips 2002a). 2002: publication of the Association of Internet Researchers guidelines on online research ethics (Ess 2002).

	Developments in internet technologies	Developments in online social research methods
2005–2009	2006: Twitter launched. 2007: iPhone launched. 2008: Google Chrome browser launched.	2005: *Virtual Methods* (Hine 2005) 2006: *International Journal of Internet Science* begins publication. 2008: *The Handbook of Online Research Methods* (Fielding, Lee and Blank 2008).
2009–2011	2010: iPad launched. 2011: number of internet users estimated as 2 billion world wide.	2009: publication of *Netnography: Doing Ethnographic Research Online* (Kozinets 2009) and *Online Research Essentials* (Russell and Purcell 2009).

The growth of the internet

Computers have been used to facilitate communication and information sharing since the early 1960s. For example, instant messaging services such as Compatible Time-Sharing System (CTSS) and Multics (Multi-plexed Information and Computing Service) were introduced, making computer-mediated communication a reality. The concept of a network of computers allowing people to communicate with each other was established in the US for Cold War military use by J.C.R. Licklider of MIT in August 1962, who described it as a 'Galactic' or 'Global' 'Information Network' (Leiner, Cerf, Clark, Kahn, Kleinrock, Lynch, Postel, Roberts and Wolff 2009). Licklider envisaged a global network of computers allowing researchers to share information and ideas. The internet was therefore developed as a research tool, although not in the first instance as a tool for social data collection.

The period from the 1960s until 1990 was a time of slow and steady growth (Lee, Fielding and Blank 2008), with the internet increasingly taking on an international, and heavily academic, character. The transformation of this network of computers into a mass medium only really happened when Tim Berners-Lee developed, and then demonstrated, the World Wide Web (WWW) in 1989 and then released it to the public in 1990, based on a text formatting system called Hypertext Mark-up Language (HTML). HTML was important because it allowed documents to be displayed almost identically on any computer world wide (Odih 2004).

From 1990, the pace of change around internet technologies acceler-
ated with the development of browsers (tools for reading and accessing
the web) such as Mosaic and then Netscape, and search tools like Archie,
WebCrawler and Alta Vista. With the launch of Internet Explorer (1995)
and Google (1997), the elements were in place to enable the web to
expand rapidly and to become a central part of people's social, cultural
and working lives.

Browsers enabled people to use the web as an information and entertainment source, while search engines allowed people to find and recall
resources. However, alongside these developments was a range of others
which expanded the internet's potential as a mode of communication.
In 1995 the first public video-conference took place, linking a technofair
in San Francisco with one in Cape Town, South Africa. However, it was
the launch of text-based Instant Messenger services in 1996 that proved
to be more influential. Text-based, real-time chat interfaces became an
extremely important form of online social interaction, and they were
quickly re-purposed by social researchers for undertaking interviews and
focus groups. It was not until the widespread dissemination of broadband
access to the internet in the early 2000s that audio and video communication channels, like Skype, began to provide a popular alternative to
text-based chat.

In 2004 O'Reilly developed the term Web 2.0 to describe a new
approach to web development and the use of the web. Theorists of
Web 2.0 stressed the constantly developing nature of the internet, the
co-productive relationship between developers and users, and the social
and user generated nature of the web. However, much of Web 2.0 was
actually built on existing tools and practices. The first weblog is credited to
Jorn Barger's Robot Wisdom website (1997), although the term was attributed to Peter Merholz, who in 1999 wrote, 'I've decided to pronounce the
word 'weblog' as 'wee-blog. Or 'blog' for short'. Similarly, it is possible to
see a wide range of other social and user driven technologies in opera-
tion before the term Web 2.0 was coined, such as SixDegrees.com which
allowed users to create profiles, list their Friends and, beginning in 1998,
surf the Friends lists (Boyd and Ellison 2007).

Web 2.0 is perhaps more usefully understood as the extension and
popularization of a variety of existing trends. Nonetheless, in the period
in which O'Reilly was theorizing this trend there was a wide range of
developments, such as the creation of Myspace (2003) and Facebook

(2004) which involved different, more communicative and more social ways of using the web. The development of social tools such as weblogs, wikis, social networking sites, microblogs and social book marking sites created new ways of using the internet to communicate and new ways of communicating. Social media typically enshrined open and many-to-many approaches to communication that allowed the creation of new social and cultural forms. Furthermore the brand names associated with these social tools (Wikipedia, Facebook, Myspace, Youtube, LinkedIn and Twitter) entered the popular, cultural and political consciousness, and have in themselves become another focus for social research.

Social tools have changed the way that people use the web, both for resource discovery and for communication. In 2009, total social network usage passed that of email (Morgan Stanley 2010), and in March 2010 Facebook overtook Google as the most popular site on the web (Dougherty 2010). This growth of social tools is already impacting on how people relate to each other, their employers, the state and even to social researchers. Central to this is the changing nature of privacy in a world where personal data is routinely made openly available and in which computational power is sufficient to extract and analyse these data (O'Hara and Shadbolt 2008). In particular, the ability to connect different data sets, to visualize them and to identify geographical information, is reshaping society's understanding of privacy and personal data. These developments offer huge opportunities for researchers (see chapter 8), but they are not without ethical challenges (see chapter 3).

While the speed of technological development has been rapid, the speed at which demographic penetration of technologies has taken place has been even more rapid. In 1994 the internet organized a relatively small network of around 3 million technologists, enthusiasts and researchers. By 2011, an estimate of the total number of internet users was around 2 billion (Econsultancy 2011). In the UK alone, 30.1 million adults use the internet every day or nearly every day (Office for National Statistics 2010). Furthermore, users are accessing and utilising the internet in new ways, including through mobile devices that allow internet use to inter-connect with offline life to ever greater extents.

However, it is important for social researchers to recognize that whilst internet use continues to grow and to penetrate new demographics, it remains far from ubiquitous. The distinction between the internet haves and have nots is often referred to as the digital divide, and the social and political implications of this new social and information hierarchy are clearly a subject for further social research over the next few years. In the UK alone there are 9.2 million adults who have never used the internet (Office for National Statistics 2010). It is also useful to explore digital exclusion and digital literacy as well as the digital divide (Hooley, Hutchinson and Watts 2010: 8). It is possible to be connected in the sense of owning a device that is capable of accessing the internet, but to still lack the skills and knowledge necessary to use the internet in ways that support social participation (Carrick-Davies 2011). Issues of digital literacy and digital inclusion are important public policy questions, and clearly shape the online populations with which researchers interact.

Wiles *et al.* argue that methodological developments often focus exclusively on a 'developed world' context (Wiles, Pain and Crow 2010). Discussion of online research methods often fails to acknowledge the developing world where demographic penetration of internet technologies is much lower. However, this does not mean that the internet is not widely used in the developing world. Indeed some figures estimate that there are more internet users (1.2 billion) in the developing world than there are in the developed world (885 million), although obviously this does not reflect the proportion of internet users in relation to overall population (International Telecommunication Union 2010). It is also important to recognize that all connectivity is not equal, and that much internet access in the developing world is through mobile devices or low bandwidth connections offering limited access.

This opening section has attempted to sketch the changes in technology associated with the internet in order to provide a context for discussion of the development of online research methods. There are a number of works that provide a more detailed understanding of the history of the technology behind the creation of the internet (Hafner and Lyons 1996; Leiner, Cerf, Clark, Kahn, Kleinrock, Lynch, Postel, Roberts and Wolff 2009; Ryan 2010). Given the close inter-relationship between technology and methodology, researchers may be interested to find out more about the personal, social and technological stories that exist behind the technologies that they are utilizing for research.

Researching online and online methods

It is important to make a distinction between research which examines the internet, and research which uses the internet to undertake online research. The focus of this book is squarely on the side of online research methods, but it is important to recognize that the two are often intertwined. Online research methods are most obviously useful when the phenomenon that is being investigated is strongly connected to the internet. As the penetration of internet technologies moves further through social demographics and becomes more embedded in a variety of everyday activities, it becomes increasingly difficult to talk meaningfully about the distinction between 'real' and 'virtual' life.

Many early social research studies investigated the social life of the internet using conventional onsite methodologies. Freeman investigated computer mediated communication and social networks using a conventional questionnaire (Freeman 1984); Finholt and Sproull looked at work-based electronic communications through creating a hard copy of all emails sent by ninety-six employees over a three-day period (Finholt and Sproull 1990); Lievrouw and Carley looked at the use of technologically mediated communication amongst scientists using literature and document analysis to build a conceptual approach (Lievrouw and Carley 1990). There is nothing fundamentally wrong with investigating online phenomena using onsite methods – indeed many researchers continue to do so – but researchers should be aware of the difference between research conducted online as opposed to that which examines the online environment.

Alongside and immediately following these onsite investigations of the internet, researchers also began to experiment with undertaking research online. Kiesler and Sproull used an email survey to look at the use of email (Kiesler and Sproull 1986); Kehoe and Pitkow saw the potential of the web for delivering surveys (Kehoe and Pitkow 1996); Foster used email for interviewing (Foster 1994); Correll began to discuss and undertake what he called 'internet ethnography' (Correll 1995); Welch and Krantz used computer-mediated communication for psychological experiments (Welch and Krantz 1996). These developments will be discussed in more depth later on in this chapter.

Online research methods as a field

Following on from these early experiments in online research, there began to be some recognition that online research methods might exist as a methodological area in their own right. As this book shows, online research methods are developed in response to a wide range of influences. Most online research methods draw heavily on a particular onsite methodological tradition. In other words, the methodology associated with online surveys is built with clear reference to the methodology of onsite, postal and telephone surveys. However, the technological possibilities of the online space also exert their own influence on methodological development. This means that as methodological approaches have moved online they have frequently had to wrestle with similar issues regardless of their epistemological basis. As will be explored in subsequent chapters. Issues such as recruitment, identity verification and the absence of visual and social cues and clues have influenced the development of a variety of social research methods as they have transferred online.

Given the range of common methodological issues that researchers have experienced online, it is possible to construct a rationale (as in this volume) for seeing online research methods as a field in its own right. However, the practice of online research methods, along with methodological thinking in the area, has been widely spread across the disciplines. The danger associated with this approach is that parallel developments can take place in disciplinary silos with little reference to relevant methodological thinking in other disciplines. A review of the literature on this subject reveals that there is considerable evidence of these kinds of parallel developments. However there has also been a range of attempts to connect up relevant literatures and to find synergy and added value in different approaches. It is therefore useful to briefly review the organizations, publications and spaces where much of the development of online research methods has taken place.

Papers about online research methods have been featured at a huge number of conferences including the Conference on Computer Supported Cooperative Work; ESRC Research Methods Festival; Human Factors in Computing Systems; iConference; International Conference on Information and Knowledge Management; the International Conference on System Sciences. Online research methods frequently inhabit the spaces between social research and technological research, and are well distributed across a range of disciplines. However, the opportunity to bring researchers together who all work on online social research, regardless of discipline, has also been of key importance. One critical conference was the World Wide Web and Contemporary Cultural Theory conference, which took place at Drake University in November 1997. This brought together many of the researchers who would go on to establish the Association of Internet Researchers (AOIR), which was launched in 2000 and has held annual conferences ever since.

As with conferences, the multi-disciplinary nature of online research methods means that research on the subject is scattered though a wider range of different academic journals. Of key importance has been the *Journal of Computer-Mediated Communication*, first published in June 1995, focusing on social research relating to the internet. Another key journal in the area is the *International Journal of Internet Science*, which began in 2006 and focuses on social and behavioural science concerned with the internet and its implications for individuals, social groups, organizations and society. Other journals that have devoted considerable coverage to online research methods include *Behaviour Research Methods, Sociological Methodology, Journal of Contemporary Ethnography, Science Computer Review, Psychological Methods, Methods of Psychological Research, Information Communication & Society, Qualitative Market Research, International Journal of Social Research Methodology, International Journal of Qualitative Methods, Journal of Mixed Methods Research, Survey Research Methods*, and *Communication Methods and Measures*. In 2008 the *International Journal of Internet Research Ethics* was launched, providing a cross-disciplinary perspective on the ethical issues emerging from online research.

The area has also been well documented in monographs and edited collections, many of which have informed the current research landscape. Of particular importance to the development of the field have been *Online Social Sciences* (Batinic, Reips and Bosnjak 2002); *Online Social Research* (Johns, Chen and Hall 2004); *Virtual Methods* (Hine 2005); *The Handbook of Online Research Methods* (Fielding, Lee and Blank 2008). More practically focused books include *The Internet Research Handbook* (O'Dochartaigh 2001); *Internet Research Methods* (Hewson, Yule, Laurent and Vogel 2002) and *Online Research Essentials* (Russell and Purcell 2009). These texts have all tried to provide an overview of the field, rather than focusing on a particular technique or methodological tradition. However, there is a vast range of other texts that has informed the thinking in the field. One element of this book is a bibliography that sets out all the literature that has been consulted in its creation. Whilst it cannot claim to be comprehensive, it does offer a broad and extensive overview of the literature on online research methods and associated areas.

As the internet is key to online research, it is unsurprising that discussion and material about online research methods is widely available online: the website Exploring Online Research Methods (Madge, O'Connor, Wellens, Hooley and Shaw 2006) offers a wide range of commentary on, and resources relating to, online research methods. Launched in 2011, The Digital Research Tools wiki (DiRT) is another highly useful website where information about technical tools that can support research are gathered together. The Digital Methods Initiative (2011) provides a useful hub and resource base for some of the more technical aspects of online research methods.

This historical summary of online research methods provides some context for the examination of research methods on which this book is focused. Developing a full understanding of the field of online research methods is difficult due to its multi- and inter-disciplinary development. To some extent this is an inevitable consequence of the way in which research is organized, as disciplinary silos explore new developments within their own arenas and only tentatively reach out to other fields. However, there is also a sense in which the development of the internet poses some challenges to existing disciplines, blurring boundaries between what is personal and political discourse, what can be described as local, specialist or mass media, and what can be seen as publication, communication and teaching and so on.

The growth of online surveys

Much of the early interest in the possibilities of online research centred around online surveys. Online surveys offered researchers an approach that was quick, low cost and easy to analyse and administer. Researchers were able to transfer methodological practices from onsite, postal and telephone surveys, and to reframe them for electronic surveys using email or web technologies. The first recorded email survey, conducted by Kiesler and Sproull in 1986, looked at electronic mail communication in organizations (Kiesler and Sproull 1986). Their research included the development of a 'reduced social cues' model. They argued that email offered an impoverished form of communication as it provides few social cues. However, they correctly concluded that the lower cost of the electronic survey was likely to lead to its increased use in the future.

The first recorded web surveys appeared around 1994 (Kehoe and Pitkow 1996), with most early online surveys produced by organizations evaluating their services and products or seeking market intelligence. For example, in 1996 the Council of American Survey Research Organizations (CASRO) undertook a survey of Fortune 2000 companies across America and found that 64% saw the potential for, and intended to commission, online surveys in the near future.

The methodological discussion around the use of online surveys also developed in the mid- to late 1990s, with numerous studies discussing and noting the research potential for this new technology (Anderson and Gansneder 1995; O'Lear 1996; Kehoe and Pitkow 1996; Schmidt 1997; Smith 1997). Researchers quickly noted that online surveys had the potential to reach large audiences at a relatively low cost and at greater speed than any earlier survey approach (Kehoe and Pitkow 1996; Schmidt 1997; Schaefer and Dillman 1998). For example, in 1999 Sheehan and McMillan conducted studies where both mail and email were used to deliver surveys. They estimated that mail surveys took an average of 11.8 days to return while the corresponding time for email surveys was 7.6 days. In fact Sheehan and McMillan's estimated online survey response times were longer than most other researchers have found. Harris, for example, found that surveys took an average of 2 to 3 days to be returned (Harris 1997).

Dillman contextualized the importance of online surveys by looking at how technological developments had previously reshaped survey methodologies (Dillman 2000). Dillman argued that online surveys built on two other significant developments in survey methodologies: random sampling (1940s) and telephone surveys (1970s). He argued that the development of online surveys was likely to be seen as the most important of these developments. Couper argued that the social implications of online surveys are just as great as the methodological ones (Couper 2000). As costs are reduced and online survey tools become easier to use, the ability to conduct a social survey becomes available to all and not just to a professional minority. Couper describes this change as a democratization of the survey. However, many professional researchers have expressed concerns about the methodological and ethical issues associated with this democratization and the corresponding danger of saturation and survey fatigue.

Many researchers have discussed whether the growth in online surveys has had a negative impact on response rates. The issue of response rates compared with traditional paper surveys was being discussed as early as 1994 (Schuldt and Totten 1994). In 1996, Comley used a multi-mode approach and compared the response rates to email and postal surveys. Because of the novelty of the email approach he achieved a 45% response rate for email and 16% for the same postal survey. However, as the use of online surveys has increased, the response rate has declined. For example, Lozar *et al.*, in their meta analysis looking at the declining response rates to surveys, found that online surveys were the worst affected survey method (Lozar, Bosnjak, Berzelak, Haas and Vehovar 2008).

The representativeness of samples was also raised as an issue as early as 1997 (Swoboda, Muehlberger, Weitkunat and Schneeweiss 1997; Schaefer and Dillman 1998; Dillman 2000). Articulating some of these method-ological concerns about sampling bias, Coomber noted that respondents to online surveys were disproportionately white, male, first world, affluent and educated (Coomber 1997). However, as the demographics of internet use have broadened this bias is unlikely to still hold true. However, this does not mean that an internet sample can be understood to be represen-tative globally. The ability to reach a global audience is highly dependent on researchers' recruitment strategies and likely to be influenced by geography, social-economic position and language amongst many other factors.

The issues of response rates and sampling demonstrate the importance of understanding methodological developments historically. As the level of penetration of the internet has grown, and increasing numbers of people have crossed the digital divide, methodologies have needed to change and develop. Online research methods have moved from inves-tigating an elite activity to a mass activity, and also have had to address the changes in culture and practice that have emerged from these social and technological developments. Many of these issues will be picked up in more depth in chapter 4.

Exploring the potential for online qualitative research

Alongside the developments in surveys, online interviews and focus groups were receiving academic interest. One important distinction that was made early on was between asynchronous interviews and focus groups which take place over time using technologies such as email and discussion boards, and synchronous interviews and focus groups in which the researcher and participant(s) interact at the same time. According to O'Connor *et al.*, asynchronous email interviews have moved into the mainstream but online synchronous interviewing remains a relatively novel and innovative approach (O'Connor, Madge, Shaw and Wellens 2008). In fact, nearly all of the early literature on the subject focused on asynchronous interviews carried out through email (Foster 1994; Gaiser 1997; Murray and Sixsmith 1998; Ward 1999).

According to Fox, online focus groups become increasingly visible in the literature from the late 1990s (Fox, Morris and Rumsey 2007; Stewart, Eckerman and Zhou 1998; O'Connor and Madge 2003; Williams 2003). Again, they mainly focused on asynchronous approaches using bulletin boards and discussion groups (Gaiser 1997; Murray 1997; Robson 1999; Ward 1999). Murray argued that focus groups could be transferred online and that many of the same principles that had underpinned onsite focus groups would continue to be useful. The methodological approach to asynchronous online focus groups were developed by Gaiser, who explored the possibilities that were offered by bulletin boards, internet relay chat (IRC) groups, multi-user dimensions (MUDs) and web conference pages as potential places to conduct focus groups. He argued that (at that time) both IRC and MUD were probably inappropriate because much of the discussion tended to be superficial and playful in nature.

The first published synchronous interviews that began to appear in the mid-1990s (Brotherson 1994; Mann and Stewart 2000) note that much of the early development of synchronous interviews focused on conferencing software (Mann and Stewart 2000; O'Connor and Madge 2001). Despite Gaiser's early reservations, Instant Messenger services such as Microsoft MSN were re-purposed for online interviewing (Luders 2004; Voida, Mynatt, Erickson and Kellogg 2004; Opdenakker 2006, Stieger and Goritz 2006).

There has also been interest in using virtual environments such as Second Life for synchronous interviews and focus groups (Gaiser 2008), and an increasing interest in the use of multi-media tools (Fielding and Lee, 2008; Fielding, 2010). These, and other more recent developments, will be picked up in chapter 5.

Doing fieldwork without a field

The third methodological tradition that this book explores is ethnographies. Hine argues that the development of online ethnographic methodologies has gone hand-in-hand with the development of the internet (Hine 2008). As the internet has been increasingly understood as a site for community and social interactions, ethnographic methodologies have provided an appropriate way to investigate and understand the lived experience of those interacting. The ethnographic investigation of the internet has been variously described. Kozinets says that the term netnography was developed by him as early as 1995 (Kozinets 2010), while Correll used the term internet ethnography (Correll 1995) and Hine referred to it as virtual ethnography. Much of this work sought to reframe existing ethnographic approaches for the online environment, whilst recognizing that radical shifts are necessary when the field of study appears as text on a screen and the group of people involved are scattered across the world (Morton 2001).

The first recorded online ethnographies began to appear in the early 1990s and were largely based on the study of discussion groups and bulletin boards, such as the ones created through Usernet (Jones 1995; Baym 1995, Correll 1995; Hauben and Hauben 1997). Unlike other online methodologies, many online ethnographers were interested largely in the new online environment from an early stage and were less interested in how these ethnographies compared to traditional offline ethnographies. This was based on an analysis that saw the online community as a new social reality. This led to a series of publications of what Hine describes as the 'cyberculture studies' (such as Silver 2000).

Increasingly, ethnographic researchers became interested in how online activity connected with offline activity. In early studies, the assumption was made that online communities could be studied in a roughly analogous way to offline communities. However, as online fieldwork methodologies and online practices developed, it became increasingly clear that ethnographers needed to explore the ways in which both online and offline communities and networks overlapped and inter-related. For example, Sade-Beck argued that focusing only on the online gives a partial understanding of how people interact (Sade-Beck 2004), while Ruthleder argues that the virtual and 'real' environments overlap and interact with one another (Ruthleder 2000).

The development of social tools and their increasing popularity has further eroded the distinction between online and offline spaces, and provided a new challenge to ethnographers. Correspondingly, a great deal of recent research has concerned the interaction of new forms of social media such as blogging (Doostdar 2004; Herring and Paolillo 2006; Hookway 2008), online gaming (Boellstorff 2006), Youtube (Liu 2007) and social network sites such as Facebook, Myspace, Twitter (Boyd and Heer 2006; Thelwall 2008) – which have created a rich new source of material and experience for ethnographers to study. These issues, along with a more detailed discussion of online ethnographies, are picked up in chapter 6.

Beginning to experiment online

Finally, this book examines the development of online experiments. Musch and Reips argue that the first web experiments were Norma Welch's 1995 experiments on auditory perception (Musch and Reips 2000), which ran simultaneously at McGill University, Montreal, Canada and Technical University, Darmstadt, Germany (Welch and Krantz 1996). However, as the experiments were combined with tutorials, there has been debate on whether these were true internet experiments. The first truly online experiment was arguably conducted by Andreas Weigend at Colorado University, who undertook three web experiments on music recognition (Weigend 1994). The first psychology web experiment to be published in an academic journal was on the determinants of female attractiveness (Krantz, Ballard and Scher 1997). This period also saw the creation of a central listing of online experiments in the Psychological Research on the Net webpage (Krantz 1995–2011).

As with other online research methods, methodological discussion around online experiments was initially focused on mapping the advantages and disadvantages of online approaches over traditional methods (Hewson, Laurent and Vogel 1996; Reips 1996a; Reips 1996b; Birnbaum 2000). For example, Hewson concluded that the main advantages of online experiments over other methods were that they were cheaper, made it easier for people to remain anonymous, and were easier for the participant because they were able to engage at their leisure. There was clearly also a number of downsides resulting from the relative loss of control for the researcher. These and other methodological issues are explored further in chapter 7.

In summary

Online research methods have now established a clear place in the social research methods canon. Researchers began to experiment online from the mid-1980s but it was only with the development of the internet as a mass form in the mid- to late 1990s that online research really began to develop as a field and to advance the methodological questions. This chapter has argued that there is a complex relationship between technology, the social use of technology and the strategies that researchers develop to examine these. This relationship forms one of the main themes of this book, as it examines the key features and debates that have emerged in the areas of online surveys, online interviews and focus groups, online ethnographies and online experiments.

Further reading

There are a number of works that provide a more detailed understanding of the history of the technology behind the creation of the internet, such as *Where Wizards Stay Up Late* (Hafner and Lyons 1996); *A Brief History of the Internet* (Leiner, Cerf, Clark, Kahn, Kleinrock, Lynch, Postel, Roberts and Wolff 2009); *A History of the Internet and the Digital Future* (Ryan 2010).

While there is no comprehensive history of the development of online research methods, there are a number of key works that provided a 'state of the nation' at key points in the field's development. These include *Online Social Sciences* (Batinic, Reips and Bosnjak 2002); *Online Social Research* (Johns, Chen and Hall 2004); *Virtual Methods* (Hine (2005); *The Handbook of Online Research Methods* (Fielding, Lee and Blank 2008).

3 Dealing with ethical issues in online research

As the amount of online social interaction has increased, social researchers have found new ways to study people online. In a book such as this it can be tempting to focus on the 'how to' technical considerations of online research, but it is also important to think about the 'whether to' and 'what to do' considerations of research ethics. One of the main considerations is to ensure that ethical practice remains up to date and relevant in a world where technology is rapidly changing and impacting on how people think about issues such as confidentiality, privacy and obtaining informed consent.

Many of the ethical issues which researchers need to consider and address prior to commencing research online require them to adopt similar ethical frameworks and practices to those employed in onsite research. However, the internet also opens up new ethical challenges and reframes existing ones. Online researchers are more readily able to bypass gatekeepers, access semi-private data, eavesdrop, deceive, re-use and re-analyse data than was previously possible. What was often difficult and time-consuming in onsite research has frequently become straightforward online.

Ethics in social science research

Considering how to conduct research in an appropriate and ethical way has always been important for social science researchers. Over recent years, in the UK and other countries, this broader raft of ethical concern and practice has become increasingly subject to formal regulation (ESRC 2010). This has meant the establishment of ethics panels built on a model borrowed from health science (Richardson and McMullan 2007), alongside the development of a variety of ethical frameworks and guides. This process has not been without its critics, and has variously been critiqued as bureaucratic, inappropriate and constraining of academic freedom (Lewis 2008; Sikes and Piper 2010; Stanley and Wise 2010).

This chapter does not seek to debate the system of ethical regulation in social research. It does however wish to make a strong argument that ethical considerations are important to social research and to social research on the internet in particular. For those new to social research ethics there are a number of useful texts which provide an overview, such as *Research Ethics for Social Scientists* (Israel and Hay's 2006); *The Handbook of Social Research Ethics* (Mertens and Ginsberg 2008); *The Student's Guide to Research Ethics* (Oliver 2010). This chapter looks at how some of the issues covered in these more general texts on research ethics are reframed in the online environment.

Ethics in online research

Discussion of research ethics can be found throughout most of the history of online research methods. There was considerable debate on the matter as early as 1996 (Allen 1996; Boehlefeld 1996; King 1996; Reid 1996; Thomas 1996). Early discussions focused on whether there was a need to develop specific guidelines for online research. Frankel and Siang argued that new guidelines were needed (Frankel and Siang 1999), whereas Walther countered this by arguing that many of the features of internet research were similar to existing offline research (Walther 2002). The work of Ess and the Association of Internet Researchers provided a series of recommendations addressing ethical decision making and internet research, which both acknowledged the similarities between online and onsite research whilst also recognizing the new challenges that the online environment presents (Ess 2002). Although they are now ten years old, the recommendations of Ess and the Association of Internet Researchers are still relevant to those undertaking online research. More recent ethical thinking has focused on researching the social networks that are facilitated by online social tools.

This chapter discusses some of the specific ethical issues and challenges which online research presents, and explores how other researchers have addressed these. These include new ethical challenges such as the way in which many web technologies create a permanent record and the subsequent possibility of connecting isolated observations or utterances to specific individuals. Many of these technologically facilitated phenomena have no offline equivalent, and raise the need to re-think existing ethical practices as they blur the distinctions in existing dichotomies such as public/private, published/unpublished, local/international and expert/

amateur (Eysenbach and Till 2001; Hudson and Bruckman 2005; Bos, Karahalios, Chávez, Poole, Thomas, and Yardi 2009).

A further challenge in relation to online research ethics is the complexity of the legal environment that regulates online activity. Navigating through this complexity can be challenging for the online researcher, especially in cases where the relevant legislative framework is more permissive than the ethical position that the researcher or their code of conduct suggests is appropriate. So, for example, it may be legally permissible for a researcher to download and analyse discussions from online public forums without the original contributors' consent, but is this approach ethical if the contributors did not post their messages with the expectation that they would be used in this way? This chapter does not set out to answer comprehensively all the ethical questions that online research raises, rather it seeks to encourage researchers to recognize the ethical pluralism that exists in online research (Ess 2002; Ess 2010) and to understand that there are multiple responses to ethical issues. Given this lack of formal absolutes it is important that researchers have the ability to adapt existing ethical approaches creatively and critically to the new social formations and research approaches that are enabled by technological changes.

case study

HIV prevention research on Facebook

Bull *et al.* utilized social media to deliver a health education intervention to young people at risk of contracting HIV (Bull, Breslin, Wright, Black, Levine and Santelli 2011). Their study targeted participants from ethnic groups with a high risk of HIV, and they were able to recruit 1588 participants aged 16 to 25. The research was conceived as a randomized controlled trial, and the health education programme was delivered through Facebook. Facebook was chosen because it was seen as being appropriate for, and well used by, the target group.

Recruitment of the first cohort of participants used a mixture of offline and online modes including community events, newspaper advertisements and personal email invitations. Respondents were screened to ensure that they met the study's eligibility requirements (which included being within the target age range and being an existing Facebook user). Eligible participants were then asked to complete an online baseline health assessment, after which they were assigned to one of two Facebook groups – the Just/Us group which was the researchers' Facebook health education programme, and 18–24 News which was a control Facebook group providing news and current affairs.

Participants were required to demonstrate their affinity to their allocated Facebook group by 'liking' it in their Facebook profile. The openness of Facebook and its status as a popular communication and networking tool amongst young people raised some additional issues in terms of the privacy/anonymity of participants. However, the implications of 'liking' one of the groups was carefully mapped by the researchers. The 'like' status meant the following in terms of the study:

- The Just/Us and 18–24 News groups were visible to and could be 'liked' by any Facebook user.
- The researchers' access to individual participants was determined by the participant's Facebook privacy settings.
- Facebook friends within an individual participant's network could see that the participant 'liked' the Facebook group.
- Individuals outside the participant's network would not know the identity of the participant – they would however be able to see the total number of Facebook users who 'like' that particular group.

Once a participant 'liked' their assigned Facebook group, they received daily updates from the research team when they logged in to their own Facebook account. In the case of the Just/Us group these provided links to more detailed information regarding health education, which the participants could choose to access or comment on.

A snowballing, respondent-driven sampling approach was used to recruit further cohorts of participants as it was thought that this approach might (and in fact did) result in higher recruitment from within the target ethnic groups. The original respondents were asked to recruit up to three of their Facebook friends to the study. Respondents recruited in this way were allocated the same Facebook group as their recruiting Facebook friend, and this snowballing technique was used to recruit up to five further cohorts of participants.

All participants undertook further online health assessments at eight weeks and six months. The study was incentivized with participants receiving giftcards at enrolment (US$15), the follow-up health assessments (US$15 each) and US$5 for each Facebook friend recruited (up to US$15).

Bull *et al.* identify a number of ethical considerations which had to be addressed during their study. These include informed consent, protection of vulnerable populations, confidentiality, data security and privacy. They highlight that whilst some of these issues were anticipated before the research began, others emerged only during the course of it.

Informed consent: This study highlights a number of issues related to participants' comprehension and engagement with the issue of informed consent. Firstly, although the researchers followed strategies aimed at facilitating comprehension of the study aims and process, they found that the participants did not particularly engage with the information provided. The researchers addressed this by making the information available in multiple locations in order that participants could access it readily. These included emailing the informed consent form to participants, attaching it to the health survey and incorporating it into the Facebook group pages. This ensured that the participants had easy access to the information and could access it whenever they chose to. Secondly, the researchers asked the participants a series of questions to ascertain whether they had read the information provided and given their informed consent before they were allowed to undertake the initial health assessment.

Protection of vulnerable groups: The target group of this study included those who were legal minors. The researchers took the decision not to require parental consent for these participants to engage with the research. The rationale for this approach was that the Facebook health education programme was addressing the same diseases for which minors can undertake health testing without the need for parental consent or knowledge. This decision and justification was considered and approved by the researchers' ethics boards. A second issue related to the protection of vulnerable groups, which Bull *et al.* considered was that of unequal access to the health education information as a result of participation in their research. The project was particularly targeting participants at a high risk of acquiring HIV who had little access to, and engagement with, HIV prevention programmes. However, those participants assigned to the control Facebook group 18-24 News did not have access to the same health education information as those assigned to the Just/Us group. To help overcome this inequality, the control group participants were invited to join the Just/Us Facebook group at the end of the research phase of the study.

Confidentiality: Bull *et al.* discuss a number of ethical issues related to confidentiality and data protection which online research, particularly that making use of social media, raise. These include the level of participant privacy afforded by the social media site itself, and that selected by the users/research participants and how these intersect with the researchers and their study. Bull *et al.* carefully considered the various Facebook relationship types and the associated levels of intimacy and confidentiality that these afforded to their research participants. They decided that the most appropriate way in which to engage participants with their health education Facebook group was through regular newsfeeds. These were sent to participants by virtue of the fact that they 'liked' the researchers' Facebook group. This decision ensured that the study did not breach or alter the participants' existing privacy levels; however, the newsfeed did provide participants with information to which they could respond via postings on the study Facebook page. Such postings were publically available and thus participants undertaking this did not remain anonymous. The researchers therefore established a posting etiquette/protocol which they shared with their participants. Throughout the study postings were monitored and the research team reserved the right to remove any postings deemed inappropriate – although they never had to invoke this.

A further data protection measure utilized by Bull *et al.* was to ensure that all data collection (for example, participant health assessments) related to their study was separate from Facebook and stored behind a firewall on a secure server at their university. This ensured that the data was not accessible to the Facebook organisation, or hackers targeting it. To increase data protection, all participant data wsa stripped of any identifiable information and allocated a study number. This was then used to access data about individual participants.

This case-study highlighted a number of ethical issues/challenges which online researchers need to consider as they design their research. However, whilst the broad ethical issues identified and discussed by Bull *et al.* may be common to much online research, the strategies they employed to address them were specific to the particular circumstances of their research. It is important that all projects identify, address, justify and reflect upon the specific ethical challenges they present, and do not merely and uncritically adopt strategies utilized by other online researches which may have been conducted in different circumstances, cultures and disciplines. Bull *et al.* also demonstrates a reflexive and recursive approach (McKee and Porter 2009) to the ethical challenges they encounter. They not only consider the ethical issues their study raised during project design and ethical review stages, but also employed strategies to address new issues that emerged as the research progressed.

The remainder of this chapter seeks to further explore a number of these key ethical issues for online researchers and to consider them from a range of alternative perspectives. However the coverage is necessarily brief and designed to map the terrain for researchers seeking to undertake online research projects.

case study

Privacy

The web, and in particular the growth of social media, has resulted in increased self-disclosure by web users who provide often detailed accounts of their 'private' life through, for example, tweets, status updates and blogs which are publically accessible to other web users. This has resulted in a blurring of the boundary between what is public and private data on the web, and puts researchers in a difficult position where they have to consider whether users' perceptions of their own privacy align with the 'public' nature of the interface they are utilising. Many online researchers have attempted to determine the status of public online data and activity by considering them to be either (i) accessible to anyone with an internet connection or (ii) data/activity that is perceived to be public by participants (even though researchers are not the intended audience) (Rosenberg 2010). Whiteman, and Langer and Beckman, have taken this stance to justify lurking in, and downloading from, postings to public discussion boards without members' knowledge (Whiteman 2010; Langer and Beckman 2005). Grodzinsky and Tavani draw upon Nissenbaum's work to examine the specific privacy issues related to blogging, and reach a similar conclusion that 'authors of (non password-protected) blogs have no reasonable expectation of their personal privacy being normatively protected' (Grodzinsky and Tavani 2010: 45; Nissenbaum 2004). Thelwall goes further, arguing that human subject standards do not apply to studies of publically available data because it is the publication, and not the person, which is being researched (Thelwall 2010).

Other researchers have taken a different position on this issue and have argued that online conversations retain elements of personal/private communication despite their openness. So Kozinets argues that researchers should be cautious when considering whether the online environment is a public or private space (Kozinets 2010). He goes on to suggest that researchers should disclose their presence during research and gain informed consent. Whiteman explores how her original ethical stance regarding the public nature of the discussion boards she was studying was challenged when the privacy settings changed part way through her research. She also goes on to explain the mixed reaction she got from the discussion board users when she provided them with links to her research findings – with some of them sharing her view that the data were public and others considering her work to be voyeuristic. Rosenberg also found a lack of agreement regarding what constituted public space amongst users of Second Life (Rosenberg 2010). Driscoll and Gregg stress how important it is for researchers to consider the specific contexts, practices and expectations of the online communities and spaces they are researching in order that they can reflect on, and justify, their ethical position (Driscoll and Gregg 2010). However, the findings of Rosenberg and Whiteman demonstrate the difficulties that exist in reaching consensus regarding what is public and what is private both amongst researchers and internet users.

Informed consent

A closely related issue to that of privacy is if, and how, researchers should negotiate and gain informed consent for research conducted online. Informed consent involves an individual being provided with, and comprehending information, about the study which is relevant to their participation and, on the basis of this information, making the decision to voluntarily participate in it. Whilst the issue of informed consent can be challenging in offline research, once again the online environment adds to the complexity. The online nature of the interaction between the researcher and potential participant, especially if text-based and asynchronous, can make it more difficult to ensure that the participant has sufficient information about the research and what it will entail. O'Connor and Madge suggest that researchers can mitigate some of these issues by providing links to further information about the research and the researchers (O'Connor and Madge 2003). Other strategies include providing a list of frequently asked questions. However, as the case-study by Bull *et al.* highlighted, participants do not always fully engage with such information when it is provided. Varnhagen *et al.* report similarities in gaining consent through online forms and through paper documents (Varnhagen, Gushta, Daniels, Peters, Parmar, Law, Hirsch, Takach and Johnson 2005). They also provide suggestions as to how to increase the accessibility and readability of online consent forms and improve participant recall of their content. However, even with such measures, it is more difficult for a researcher to confirm that the participant is able to give consent and, for example, ensure that they are not from a vulnerable group. Grimes discusses a range of issues surrounding informed consent and children's comprehension of privacy and terms of service statements related to gaming sites (Grimes 2008). However, many of the issues Grimes raises are equally applicable to adult internet users and include:

- Difficulties in navigating the ambiguous boundary between public and private.
- Lack of recognition that the gaming site/online environment being used is a commercial entity.
- Lack of understanding of the ways in which their data and online behaviour could be used (for example, being sold as market research reports).
- Terms of service and privacy policies often hidden within the site, densely worded and in legal language which is not accessible to the target audience.
- Different ethical practices between market researchers and academic researchers.

Online spaces and communities comprise a range of individuals with varying agendas and levels of participation, and this diversity can complicate the negotiation of access and informed consent. Shirky describes how online social interactions tend to follow a power law distribution. In other words, in online communities there are typically a small number of participants who are very active and a large number who are almost inactive but who still remain a part of the community (Shirky 2003; 2009). In such circumstances identifying and gaining informed consent from all of these individuals may be unrealistic (if not impossible) and some researchers have instead sought consent from gatekeepers prior to undertaking research (Barratt and Lenton 2010; Im, Chee, Tsai, Bender and Lim 2007).

For some research it may be that seeking consent from participants, whether directly or through a gatekeeper, may have a negative effect on the phenomena under study, either by changing participants' behaviour or because the researcher is not likely to be welcomed by the community or participants they are studying (Chen, Hall and Johns 2004). In these situations some researchers (Whiteman 2010) have lurked and observed behaviour without the knowledge of the users, and others (Lamb 1998) have utilized deception as part of their research approach. The issue of deception, whether in online or offline research, always raises serious ethical concerns for researchers. Whitty explores the ethical issues associated with both lurking and deception in online dating sites, and concludes that in that particular context deception which includes posing as a potential date is not acceptable (Whitty 2004). Nagel *et al.* further explored the ethical issues associated with online deception. In their study they created a virtual student, through whom they facilitated specific learning interventions during an online postgraduate course (Nagel, Blignaut and Cronjé 2007). This research was approved through their institution's research ethics approval process, and they explore the issues they addressed as well as the mixed reaction they encountered from the students when the real nature of the virtual student was revealed at the end of the course. This included both a feeling of betrayal at the deception, as well as an acknowledgement of the role that the virtual student had played in students' learning.

Anonymity and confidentiality

In offline research, anonymity and confidentiality are frequently used to protect participants' identities. Anonymity refers to a situation when no one, including the researcher, can relate a participant's identity to any information related to the project. Confidentiality describes the situation where the researchers know the participant's identity but have undertaken not to reveal it to others. Whilst the same concepts apply in online research, the nature of the internet and the way in which online data is collected may inadvertently mean a researcher cannot offer participants the same level of anonymity or confidentiality. For example, a researcher running an online survey may not need to collect any personal information about their participants, and thus believe that their survey is completely anonymous. However if the survey platform they are using collects users' IP addresses, then there is a theoretical possibility that a participant's response could be linked back to them. Whilst the chance of this happening may appear small, it has been a particular issue which researchers such as Comber – who undertook online research into illicit drug activities (Comber 1997) – have had to contend with in order that they could assure their participants that the data they provided could not be utilized by enforcement agencies.

While it can be difficult to guarantee absolute anonymity, the issue of confidentiality is even more challenging when undertaking research online. Even though individuals' identities can be disguised through the use of pseudonyms, it may be relatively straightforward to re-identify individuals. The power of tools such as Google means that any direct quotation used in the dissemination of research findings can be easily traced back to its original context. In addition, it may be possible to re-identify individuals by triangulating data from various online sources, as was demonstrated by Sweeney who used zip code, date of birth and gender to identify the Governor of Massachusetts' health record from a supposedly anonymized publically available dataset (Sweeney 2000). Further issues of confidentiality and anonymity specifically related to the re-use and archiving of qualitative data for secondary analysis are discussed by Parry and Mauthner (Parry and Mauthner 2004). These include the challenge for participants in giving their informed consent for research which extends beyond the original study.

The ethical frameworks used to address privacy, consent and anonymity have been considered more broadly by Carusi and O'Riordan, who reflect upon the relational aspects of internet research (Carusi 2008; O'Riordan 2010). O'Riordan questions the pressure which researchers face to conform to human-subject models of informed consent and anonymity. Carusi takes the discussion of the ethics of confidentiality and privacy further to distinguish between the conceptions of 'thin' and 'thick' identity (Carusi 2008: 41). She describes thin identity as 'the identity of a particular individual as a re-identifiable entity', whereas thick identity refers to 'that individual's experience of their own personhood, their own subjective or psychological sense of who they are'. She goes on to consider the role that researchers may play in mediating and representing participants' identities, and the extent to which this may align with the participants' own 'thick' identity.

Legal issues

Legal and ethical considerations are frequently intertwined and considered together during the process of ethical review of research. Generally, it would not be considered ethical for a researcher to undertake research that involves breaking the law but, as has already been noted, there may be situations where the law permits something which lies outside accepted ethical standards. In online research the situation once again becomes more complex, and researchers need to be aware of the legislation surrounding copyright, intellectual property, data ownership, transfer and storage. This is further complicated when online research is international and researchers are potentially operating in other or multi- jurisdictions. Charlesworth provides a helpful exploration of the key legal issues involved in conducting online research, and identifies some of the strategies that researchers can use to mitigate these legal risks (Charlesworth 2008). His chapter particularly considers the UK legal framework. Lipinski addresses legal issues, particularly negligence, for researchers utilizing data from online forums and postings (Lipinski 2008). Lipinski's work particularly considers these issues from a US perspective.

Another legal aspect which arises in relation to online research are the contractual Terms of Service (ToS) to which online participants agree when they sign up to online communities, social networks and games sites. In many instances the detail of the ToS may result in users transferring some of their legal rights to site owners. For example, in 2009 there was considerable uproar when Facebook changed elements of its ToS in relation to content ownership (CNN 2009). Online researchers need to consider who owns the data that they wish to utilize in their study, and to recognize that the ToS for some online sites may restrict or specifically prevent them from utilizing data for research purposes. Reynolds and De

Zwart address this issue in their examination of the ToS of a number of Massively Multi-player Online Role Play Games (MMOs), and consider the implications of these for ethnographic researchers who participate as players in these games (Reynolds and De Zwart 2010). Although the issues briefly outlined here intersect with many of the ethical issues already discussed, including privacy and consent, they bring in additional dimensions which it is important for the online researcher to be aware of if they are to mitigate legal risks.

Participant vulnerability

One of the particular advantages of online research is that it enables researchers to access isolated and hard-to-reach populations. Online communities often gather around sensitive issues, and this may also result in their being considered vulnerable, such as the cancer patients studied by Im et al. (Im, Chee, Tsai, Bender and Lim 2007). In other cases it may be that vulnerable participants are recruited because they form part of the wider population being studied (such as children who participate in online game sites). Existing mechanisms for participant and researcher protection may not be sufficient in the online environment because, as Stern notes, 'given both the nature of online communication and research, those who study internet users and communities may find themselves particularly likely to come across distressing information in their research' (Stern 2003). Whilst it is not possible to plan for all situations, it is important that researchers have considered in advance how they will deal with distressing information and/or vulnerable participants. Their strategy will need to be documented and considered by an ethics approval process prior to the commencement of research. If appropriate this information should also be shared with participants. Nevertheless, even when researchers have considered such issues in advance, dealing with them is likely to be difficult and throw up new challenges. Stern and Seko provide examples of the approaches online researchers have taken to participant disclosures related to self-harm/suicide (Seko 2006).

A different perspective on considerations related to participant vulnerability is provided by O'Connor (O'Connor 2010). He discusses the responsibilities that researchers who are undertaking health-related research have in addressing the promulgation of incorrect medical information in online communities. He suggests approaches that researchers can adopt in such circumstances, but it should be noted that researchers need to have appropriate specialist expertise to identify and address the risks that such situations pose.

In summary

Ethics are situated and contextualized within research design and methodology – but this doesn't give researchers free rein to justify any approach, nor does it mean that broader ethical frameworks are not useful. All ethical codes are fluid and dynamic, and perhaps no more so than with online research where the fast pace of technological advancement potentially magnifies this dynamism. Thus the particular ethical decisions and justifications which other researchers have convincingly made even in the relatively recent past may no longer be appropriate due to, for example, changes in the ways in which users interact with online technologies (Boellstorff 2006) or changes in system architecture (Whiteman 2010). Online researchers also have to consider and negotiate the intersection of legal and ethical frameworks, and these can redefine and reshape ethical concepts such as privacy, consent and confidentiality.

Further reading

More comprehensive coverage of the topics raised here is provided in a number of publications specifically addressing the issue of online ethics. These include *Digital Media Ethics (Digital Media and Society)* (Ess 2009); 'The ethics of internet research' (Eynon, Fry and Schroeder 2008); *The Ethics of Internet Research* (McKee and Porter 2009); the *International Journal of Internet Research Ethics* (http://ijire.net/). There are also articles addressing specific disciplinary approaches such as psychology, 'Practical advice for conducting ethical online experiments and questionnaires for United States psychologists' (Barchard and Williams 2008), and ethnography, 'My profile: The ethics of virtual ethnography' (Driscoll and Gregg 2010). In addition there are forums such as the Association of Internet Researchers wiki that provide opportunities for researchers to debate the specific issues and challenges related to undertaking research online.

4 Online surveys

The use of online questionnaires to gather survey data has become ubiquitous. They offer huge value to researchers in terms of cost, speed of data collection and analysis, and access to respondents. Given these advantages it is unsurprising that their use extends far beyond the world of academic research. Web users are likely to encounter online surveys frequently, and many of these will have been issued by service providers or marketing companies rather than academic researchers. This experience may lead some web users to consider most online surveys as little better than spam. For this reason academic researchers have to ensure that their surveys exemplify good practice; they should be aware that engaging a target population in an online survey may not be a simple or straightforward task. This chapter explores some of the issues surrounding online surveys, provides readers with an overview of the method, and a range of practical advice on how to develop effective surveys, maximize response rates and minimize dropout rates and missing data.

case study

Using online surveys to investigate childhood cancer survivors

Cantrell and Lupinacci undertook research with early childhood cancer survivors in order to examine how the experience of cancer had impacted on their physical and psychosocial characteristics, and to explore their quality of life (Cantrell and Lupinacci 2007; Cantrell and Lupinacci 2008). They chose to undertake the study using an online survey and they discuss a range of reasons for doing this – such as cost-effectiveness, decreased data collection time (compared to other methods) and increased accuracy of data collection. However, they argue that the methodology was particularly appropriate because it enabled them to reach a 'hidden' population who may not wish to identify themselves openly as cancer survivors. Furthermore, the respondents were geographically dispersed and hard-to-reach using conventional survey techniques, as there was no central database of the population. Because their target population was young adults (aged 22–28), the researchers were able to assume a familiarity with using the web.

Cantrell and Lupinacci developed a pilot online questionnaire and trialled it with ten healthy adults. Individuals who participated in the pilot were asked to say how long the questionnaire took to complete and to make suggestions to improve usability. Following the pilot, some modifications were made to the survey. It was then launched and advertised on six websites used by childhood survivors of cancer. The articles posted on these websites included an introduction to the research protocol, a pledge of anonymity, the researchers' email addresses, information about the investigators' research and clinical nursing experience background, and a direct link to the online questionnaire.

The questionnaire was designed to take around 15 minutes to complete and included 167 questions, which is arguably more than would be ideal. Participants were required to complete every question to try to reduce missing data. However, after 16 responses the researchers recognized that a long questionnaire entirely comprising mandatory questions was likely to lead to increased dropout rates. The researchers chose to relax this requirement for all subsequent participants, allowing them to skip questions as they chose. Cantrell and Lupinacci considered whether the missing data could have been minimized by making fewer questions optional or by changing the nature of some of the questions that were asked. However, the study was dealing with a sensitive topic and they reflected that if some questions were mandatory they might have resulted in emotional distress to some participants.

This case-study (as with others in this book) is not advanced as a flawless exemplar of good practice, but rather shown as a concrete example from which researchers can learn and adapt for their own purposes. Indeed Cantrell and Lupinacci are largely concerned with considering what methodological learning can be extracted from their experience (Cantrell and Lupinacci 2007). Furthermore, in 2008 Larew constructively critiqued a number of areas of Cantrell and Lupianacci's methodology, including their approach to sampling and the decision to make questions compulsory, as well as reflecting on how changes in technology open up further possibilities for enhanced survey design (Larew 2008; Cantrell and Lupinacci 2007). However, Cantrell and Lupinacci's experience remains interesting, particularly because it illustrates the way in which the study's methodology was built out of the research questions and closely related to the needs of the target population. Furthermore, the willingness to pilot, adapt and reflect on the methodology during and after the study demonstrates a critical reflexivity that researchers working with the constantly shifting world of online research methods are likely to need.

case study

Survey design

Whilst this chapter focuses on using survey methodologies online, it is important to recognize that there are strong continuities between online and onsite research. Most of the basic principles of survey-based methodologies remain the same when they move online. Rather than discuss the basics of survey design, this chapter focuses on how these issues are recontextualized by moving the survey methodology online. Those new to survey-based methods might want to read this chapter alongside a more general book such as *Survey Research Methods* (Babbie 1990); *Conducting Survey Research in the Social Sciences* (Newman and McNeil 1998); *Survey Research Methods (Applied Social Research Methods)* (Fowler 2008). Any of these books (alongside many others) will provide the reader with a solid introduction to methods of survey-based data collection and analysis.

It is perhaps worth beginning by providing definitions for some key terms that will be used in this chapter:

- **Surveys:** research methods which researchers can use to collect data. They can be either quantitative or qualitative in focus, or a mixture of the two.
- **Questionnaires:** tools or instruments which researchers use to undertake a survey. They usually comprise a series of questions or stimuli for response.
- **Populations:** the total group of people that are being studied. Researchers will commonly be unable to interact with everyone

being studied (the population), and will therefore need to work with a sample.

- **Samples:** part of a population that is examined for the purpose of drawing inferences about the population as a whole. Quantitative researchers may use statistical techniques to determine their sample and to analyse the data they gather.
- **Recruitment:** the ways in which participants are encouraged to take part in a survey.
- **Response rates:** the number of people who participate in a survey in relation to the number of people in the sample. This is often expressed as a percentage.

These definitions are basic, but it is recognized that online research methods cut across a range of disciplinary and methodological backgrounds, so it is useful to establish some core definitions. These definitions can be found alongside a range of other terms in the glossary associated with this book.

When to use an online survey?

Developing the appropriate methodology(ies) to address a particular set of research questions is one of the most critical decisions that a researcher makes. If a survey-based methodology is determined to be suitable, the researcher then has a range of decisions to make about the most appropriate way to collect data, engage participants and manage the survey. Surveys can be conducted face-to-face, by post, by telephone and by a range of other mechanisms. The decision to use an online survey must therefore be considered carefully and weighed up against the alternatives. The purpose of this chapter is not to encourage researchers to use online surveys regardless of context, but rather to help guide their appropriate use.

Despite sounding this note of caution, online surveys are becoming more frequent compared to alternative survey methodologies and this is likely to continue as the demographic penetration of the internet increases. It is therefore useful to consider some of the advantages and disadvantages of online surveys. Madge et al. argue that online surveys have the following advantages (Madge, O'Connor, Wellens, Hooley and Shaw 2006):

- Speed and volume of data collection (Fleming and Bowden 2009).
- Savings in costs.
- Flexible design.
- Data accuracy.
- Access to research populations.
- Anonymity.
- Respondent acceptability.

Many of these advantages are discussed in the Cantrell and Lupinacci case-study (Cantrell and Lupinacci 2007; Cantrell and Lupinacci 2008). However, online surveys are clearly not appropriate in all circumstances and with all populations. Furthermore, there are a number of downsides associated with online surveys. These are also discussed by Madge *et al.*, who note the following:

- Sample bias.
- Measurement error.
- Non-response bias.
- Length, response and dropout rates.
- Technical problems.
- Ethical issues.

This chapter returns to some of these issues in more detail later on. The key sampling issues are, however, whether the population that can be accessed using an online survey is different to that which can be reached using other survey approaches (sample bias), and whether respondents behave in a different way because they are participating online as compared to another survey method (measurement error). There is a range of potential technical and ethical issues that are associated with the online environment (discussed in more depth in chapters 2 and 3). However, many of the advantages and disadvantages associated with online surveys are both contested and dynamic. As discussed in chapters 1 and 2, the online environment continues to change and develop as more users are attracted to it, technologies change and as the cultural position of the internet itself shifts. Researchers are likely to need to continue to innovate in the methodologies that they use in order to continue to address and respond to these changes. There are no rules about when an online survey should be used as opposed to some other form of survey. The task is, as ever, to use methodologies that are appropriate for the research questions and populations that you are examining. Obviously if most of your population are not internet users then an online method is clearly inappropriate, but most of the time the issues are likely to present in more subtle ways. For example, if the verification of identity is an important aspect of your research then a conventional online survey might present problems.

Discussing the phenomenon of online identity manipulation, Roberts and Parks question whether we can trust the identities that people convey through online personas (Roberts and Parks 2001). However, the idea that an offline identity exists that is more real than an individual's online identity has been frequently challenged (Turkle 1999; Bowker and Tuffin 2003; Valkenburg and Peter 2008). A related issue is whether researchers are more able to judge the trustworthiness of participants in a face-to-face environment. Hewson *et al.* argue that onsite a researcher is able to pick up on a variety of visual and social clues to judge the trustworthiness of the response (Hewson, Yule, Laurent and Vogel 2003). However, research around online identity suggests that different but equivalent clues exist to signify authenticity, identity and trustworthiness (Toma and Hancock 2009; Mislove, Viswanath, Gummadi and Druschel 2010; Shin and Kim 2010). So, even if a research question requires a mechanism for identity verification and assessing trustworthiness, it does not necessarily answer the question as to whether to use online or onsite methods. In the case of an online survey, identity might be verified through the development of a password-protected site and the issuing of passwords. However, the use of passwords does not 'solve' the problem of identity verification any more than physically meeting someone guarantees their truthfulness, but careful methodological thinking can aid the creation of an appropriate tool for data gathering and put in place processes that minimize the likelihood of receiving problematic responses to surveys.

The question of whether to use online or onsite methodologies is also becoming increasingly blurred with the growth in power and availability of mobile devices which make it possible to blend onsite and online approaches together. Face-to-face surveys are often conducted using a tablet PC, with results being sent to a database during the course of the interaction. This makes it increasingly possible to blend together the results that are generated through onsite and online surveys, but what are the methodological issues in doing this? Converse *et al.* undertook a mixed postal-/web-based survey and reported increased response rates (Converse, Wolfe, Huang and Oswald 2008); this was confirmed by Dillman *et al.* who combined together a wider range of different survey methods (Dillman, Phelps, Tortora, Swift, Kohrell, Berck and Messer 2009). However, Sax *et al.* and Dillman *et al.* also concluded that there were some differences in the way people responded to the different modes of survey (Sax, Gilmartin and Bryant 2003). How people respond to online surveys in comparison to other kinds of survey has not been comprehensively mapped and is likely to remain dynamic. However, some research argues that web-based surveys have lower response rates (Shih and Fan 2008), but deliver less missing data (Dolnicar, Laesser and Matus 2009). In contrast to this, several studies which have investigated this issue have found that there are few differences in the way people respond to different survey modes (Arnau, Thompson and Cook 2001; Gosling, Vazire, Srivastava and John 2004; Fleming and Bowden 2009).

Online surveys and instrument design

Following the decision to utilize an online survey, the next step is to design an instrument that can be used to collect data. There are a number of challenges which need to be considered whilst developing an online survey, and Couper provides a comprehensive overview (Couper 2008).

Issues associated with online survey design can broadly be described as relating to either the questionnaire's *accessibility* or its *usability*. Accessibility describes elements of the design that either prevent, limit or enable the whole population responding to a survey. Accessibility issues commonly relate to disability or to the challenges of responding to a survey from a range of different platforms with different technical specifications. Usability relates to the design features that the respondent encounters whilst they are trying to assess and respond to the survey.

Poorly designed websites can pose considerable barriers for individuals with disabilities. Well-designed sites take account of the fact that people might be accessing the site using screen readers, or that they may seek to change background colour or increase font size to enhance readability. There is an extensive literature on web accessibility, and it is probably worth consulting a basic introductory text such as the W3C's accessibility materials (W3C 2010). Accessibility is also an important consideration when thinking about the selection of an appropriate tool to use for your research. The issues of ensuring access to online surveys for people with disabilities often require similar solutions to more general issues about accessibility relating to different operating systems, browsers and devices.

There are tensions between the functionality and the accessibility of all resources on the web. Broadly speaking, the more things a website/online survey can do, the more problems that people will encounter in accessing it. People access websites from a wide range of different technical environments, and the variations that exist in browsers, operating systems, screen size and bandwidth will mean that the experience of the designer of the survey is unlikely to be the same as the experience of the respondent. During the survey design this variability can be explored through piloting in a variety of environments and enabling flexibility and user configurability. Crawford, McCabe and Pope recognized this and called for the creation of survey design standards (Crawford, McCabe and Pope 2005). They argued that there were four main areas in which researchers might want to establish clearer standardization: screen design; questionnaire writing; respondent communication and process standards. This attempt moves beyond merely ensuring accessibility, and towards developing enhanced usability for respondents to web questionnaires.

Despite the arguments made by Crawford, McCabe and Pope, it is difficult to fully standardize the area of web usability. Individuals' preferences in the use of web resources vary, and thus specifying design features which facilitate increased engagement can be challenging to render as a set of standards. There is a considerable body of research and practice in the area of enhancing web usability. Offering a practical introduction to this area, Krug emphasises the importance of paying attention to existing conventions (what do everyone else's online surveys look like?) and undertaking formative piloting of the instrument during its development (Krug 2005). But there are a number of established areas to pay attention to in the design of online surveys:

- **Transparency:** Respondents should be able to easily ascertain the purpose, rationale and context of any survey they participate in. In practice this means that background information such as who is undertaking the survey, who is funding it, what the main research questions are, how data will be stored and where findings will be reported should all be available to respondents. A short welcome screen providing a summary of the project, with an associated box to indicate consent, is also a key element of this.

- **Consistency:** Online questionnaires should be designed to be internally consistent. Respondents are likely to find changes in font, colour and navigation disorientating. Key to this is the importance of limiting the range of question types used across a questionnaire. Each question type that is introduced (such as multiple choice, multiple answer, ranking) presents respondents with a new usability challenge. Further discussion of different question types can be found in Dillman, Tortora and Bowker, Best and Krueger, and Healey. (Dillman, Tortora and Bowker 1998; Best and Krueger 2004; Healey 2009). In general, choose simple question types which users are able to parse in a single glance and avoid the proliferation of question types. Crucially, there is value in piloting a questionnaire before launch and watching someone completing it. Observation of this kind is a very powerful tool for identifying which questions are likely to pose usability challenges.

- **Brevity:** The flexibility and low cost of the online form allows researchers the potential to create very long questionnaires. However, many researchers argue that shorter online questionnaires receive higher response rates and less dropout than longer ones (Deutskens, de Ruyter, Wetzels and Oosterveld 2004; Ganassali 2008; Galesic and Bosnjak 2009). Given this, there are clearly strong reasons to try and ensure that questionnaires are kept short and that appropriate use is made of routing questions to ensure that respondents are answering only the questions that they need to. Dillman, Tortora and Bowker argue that the inclusion of a progress indicator to inform respondents about how much of the survey they have completed will reduce dropout rates. However these positive effects are likely to be realized only when the progress bar is an accurate indicator of the amount of time taken (Yan, Conrad, Tourangeau and Couper 2010).

- **Respondent autonomy:** Respondents to online questionnaires are usually giving their time for free and without any promise of personal advantage. Given this, it is important that the experience is a positive one. Furthermore, researchers have a duty to conduct research in an ethical way without compulsion. In practice this means that making questions compulsory should be avoided where possible. In addition, it should usually be possible to exit the questionnaire whilst ensuring that the data you have submitted is included in the survey. These issues of respondent autonomy clearly need to be balanced with concerns about missing data. However, it is also important to recognize that respondent desire for autonomy is likely to increase where sensitive subjects are being dealt with.

Choosing a tool to deliver the survey

There is a vast array of different tools that deliver online surveys. In the early days of using online surveys, researchers often had to struggle to access online survey tools or to build their own. Madge *et al.* include a detailed technical guide that takes researchers through the process of crafting an online survey from scratch (Madge, O'Connor, Wellens, Hooley and Shaw 2006). Increasingly, however, it is unnecessary to build a bespoke survey tool since there is a growing range of purpose-built tools which researchers with basic IT literacy can use effectively. It is not possible to provide a list of such tools because the market is shifting quickly – new tools are developed regularly and old ones fall out of use. A judicious use of a search engine using 'online survey tools' will generate numerous options for you to investigate, many of which will be free or low cost, and it can be useful to look for review sites to help in your decision making. There is also a number of sources that will provide more academic discussions of survey tool selection (Wright 2005; Madge, O'Connor, Wellens, Hooley and Shaw 2006; Kacmirek 2008). If you have access to technical support (for example, through a university) it may be useful to explore and consider any options that are actively supported. However, in choosing a survey tool it may be useful to consider some of the following issues:

- **Accessibility and usability:** These issues have already been discussed above, but it is important that they are attended to at the point at which a tool is being selected.
- **Analysis tools:** Does the tool offer any analysis functionality? This may not be necessary if you are likely to move the data into another format for analysis, but such functionality can be useful to gain a quick overview of progress whilst the survey is ongoing.
- **Configurability:** How much control is it possible to exert over the way that a particular tool looks/operates. This may relate to basic issues such as colour and font, but is also likely to be critical when looking at issues such as page design and routing of questions.

- **Data security:** You have ethical, and possibly legal, responsibilities to ensure that your data is kept in a secure fashion. Examining the data security of any tool that you select is therefore crucial.
- **Ease of use/support:** There are big advantages to choosing a tool that you can use easily yourself without the requirement for technical support.
- **Export formats:** Does the tool allow you to export data into the format in which you will analyse it – for example, SPSS or Excel?
- **Question type:** What range of questions do different tools offer, and do these question type match with your needs?
- **Vendor limits:** Some vendors place limits on things such as the maximum number of questions, amount of responses or file size available. Often these limits can be removed by paying for an advanced license. However, it is important to investigate the limits that are being placed and match them to your needs.
- **Verification tools:** Does the tool offer any way to verify identity or manage spam? There are a variety of approaches, including the issuing of passwords or the verification against email addresses or other online accounts such as Google or Facebook.

Once a tool has been chosen it is recommended you pilot it to ensure that it is able to deliver all of the functionality that is required.

Sampling and recruitment

For many researchers, understanding sampling issues and developing appropriate recruitment strategies is likely to be key to the successful adoption of online methods. Some issues relating to sampling and recruitment have already been discussed, including the need to craft carefully the research questions and select the target population, as have the issues around verifying identity. However, just as problematic as verifying the identity of a particular respondent is the difficulty of establishing a clear picture of the population that can, or might, view the survey. For researchers coming from a quantitative tradition, this lack of clarity can present serious difficulties. However, as with many issues relating to online research methods these issues are not unique to the online environment, they are just exacerbated by it. It has always been possible to conduct research on 'broad and diffuse populations' (Couper 2007: S88), and it has always been challenging to construct sampling strategies in relation to these groups. One of the effects of moving these kinds of surveys online is that any attempt to recruit widely runs the risk of exceeding the population altogether by, for example, engaging respondents from across the world in research that was designed for a particular national context. However, Norman and Russell argue that this 'pass-along effect' should not always be seen as negative and may, with careful consideration, intentionally be incorporated into the sampling strategy (Norman and Russell 2006). It is important to recognize that the ability to access a wide population through the dissemination of surveys via online networks also offers considerable advantages, such as making traditionally hard-to-reach groups more accessible (Dodd 1998: 63). Furthermore, it is also possible to use statistical strategies such as weighting to reduce bias in some cases (Best and Krueger 2004).

The problem with defining a web population is that there is no central database of online identities of the kind that is provided (in the UK and many other countries) by the electoral roll. In addition, it is frequently difficult to link what online information does exist to other information about an individual, such as their geographical position or demographics, although (as is discussed in chapter 8) this is becoming increasingly possible. In certain contexts, such as surveys of single organizations or networks, it is possible that, with the collaboration of a gatekeeper, researchers will be able to gain a clearer picture of the population. In these cases a wide range of more conventional sampling approaches and statistical techniques becomes useful. In fact, where survey responses can be joined up with existing data that is held on individuals, either by the researcher or on the internet, a range of analytical possibilities are opened up. However, the process of mashing datasets together is ethically challenging, especially if some of this data is harvested from the internet without the permission of the individual. In particular, it is likely to challenge anonymity unless very carefully handled (O'Hara and Shadbolt 2008).

Regardless of the approach that is taken in constructing a sample frame, researchers are likely to experience challenges in recruitment and ensuring a good response rate. One useful element of conducting an online survey is that normally the turnaround time between sending out the survey and receiving responses is relatively short. Crawford, Couper and Lamias suggest that if people are going to complete a web-survey they will do so in the first few hours or days of receiving it (Crawford, Couper and

Lamias 2001). However, it has also been found that increasing response rates can be achieved by follow-up reminders (Schaefer and Dillman 1998; Crawford, Couper and Lamias, 2001). Response rates can also be improved with introductory letters or emails (Porter and Whitcomb 2003), by recommendation from a trusted intermediary (Fang, Shao and Lan 2009), or by increasing the social presence of the researchers in the survey (Best and Krueger 2004). Madge *et al.* have constructed a checklist based on a synthesis of the literature around response rates to online surveys (Madge, O'Connor, Wellens, Hooley and Shaw 2006).

Improve response rates: a checklist (Madge et al.)

1 Send introductory letter outlining project and estimated time needed to complete the questionnaire.
2 Include an institutional/official website to help validate researchers' identity.
3 Provide clear instructions on how to complete the questionnaire.
4 Request personal information at the start of the questionnaire rather than the end.
5 Use simple questionnaire format and avoid unnecessary graphics.
6 Avoid grid questions, open-ended questions and requests for email addresses.
7 Design the survey so that it takes approximately 10 minutes to complete.
8 Do not include more than 15 questions.
9 Send one or two follow-up reminders.
10 Include 'social presence' (information to increase trust in the researchers) or missing data messages (thanking participants for completing the survey and informing them about their progress within it) to reduce item non-response.
11 Emphasise confidentiality.

In summary

Online surveys offer researchers a powerful tool with many advantages. It is anticipated that as the social penetration of the internet increases, and online and mobile technologies continue to become more embedded in the lives of the majority of people in the developed world and to a sizable global minority, the utility of online surveys will continue to grow. However, the use of online surveys is not without challenges in areas such as identity verification, sampling and representativeness. For those working in the quantitative tradition, these issues may pose considerable concerns. Thankfully there is a lively and ever growing research literature which is examining these issues and developing strategies to address them. In general, as with other online research methods, online surveys should not be viewed as a panacea. Rather, online surveys need to be used carefully and critically and combined with onsite and postal approaches where appropriate.

Further reading

There has been a considerable amount of energy devoted to the discussion and exposition of online survey-based methods. *Designing Effective Web Surveys* (Couper 2008) provides a good overview of the area, as does *Internet, Mail, and Mixed-Mode Surveys: The Tailored Design Method* (Dillman, Smyth and Christian 2008). A very useful practical guide is *Successful Online Surveys* (Healey 2009), which is available online for free, while *Don't Make Me Think* (Krug 2005) provides a solid grounding in the web-usability issues that are central to effective online survey design.

5 Online interviews and focus groups

As the previous chapter discussed, online surveys have been widely picked up by social scientists. However, the adoption of online qualitative techniques, such as interviews and focus groups, has been much more limited. This chapter explores these online qualitative techniques and provide an introduction to their use.

The chapter examines some of the key decisions that researchers wishing to undertake interviews and focus groups will have to make. These include considering the relative merits of synchronous, asynchronous, text-based, audio, video, one-to-one and group-based interviews.

case study

Using email as a medium for qualitative interviewing

Busher and James undertook two distinct qualitative studies with tertiary educators (Busher 2001; James 2003). They both used email as the medium for the interviews and later took the opportunity to reflect jointly on how this medium impacted on their studies (James and Busher 2006). In their methodological reflections they suggest that, while email interviewing presents the researcher with a number of challenges, it also offers considerable benefits and that there is value in continuing to refine and develop the methodology.

Busher's 2001 study focused on ten adult educators who were undertaking a doctorate at an English university. The educators were studying part-time, whilst working in a wide range of different environments across the world, with many using English as a second or third language. James's 2003 study examined the professional identity of psychology lecturers in UK higher education. Again participants were dispersed and, as with Busher's study, the process of interviewing was asynchronous and allowed to unfold over an extended period of time.

Busher and James both utilized email as the main medium for their interviews. They sought a 'research method that could capture and reflect narrative accounts of participants' experiences and provoke in-depth reflection of their understandings of their developing professional experiences and identities' (James and Busher 2006: 404). The researchers considered alternative mediums such as face-to-face qualitative interviewing, which was impractical because of the location of participants, and telephone interviewing which was also rejected for practical reasons (for example, time zones) as well as for methodological ones (the belief that it would elicit short answer responses rather than the deep, reflective accounts that these projects required).

Email interviewing was therefore chosen because it overcame issues of distance and time difference, and because the asynchronous, iterative nature of the exchange was believed to facilitate reflection by participants. The researchers also decided that the one-to-one mode facilitated by email was appropriate to their research objectives in contrast to a group approach that might have been facilitated by some kind of online discussion forum.

In their studies of 2001 and 2003 respectively, James and Busher both chose to send questions one at a time to participants. This meant that the interviews took place over an extended period of time, and that participants had the opportunity to reflect, consider and potentially to redraft their answers. This meant that the kind of data generated was considerably different to that generated in a conventional interview. On one hand participants had the opportunity to be more considered and to give longer responses if they wished. The process of interviewing also interweaved with the participant's day-to-day life. On the other hand there are dangers of misunderstandings arising, the focus of the interview being lost and participants dropping out (either temporarily or permanently). James and Busher both took active strategies to manage some of these issues by contracting participants at the start of the interview (setting out the number of questions, expected response times and other processes related to the interview) and using a variety of prompts during the interview process, such as 'Haven't heard from you in a while. I wondered if you still wished to continue the interview?' However, despite these strategies the process of email interviewing still proved to be longer and more difficult than expected.

These researchers' experiences demonstrate the complex interaction that exists between technology, methodology, the participants, their context and the research objectives. The data that emerged from both of their studies would have been different if they had changed any one element of their study. The use of email interviews was useful in eliciting substantial, reflective responses to interviewers' questions, and in allowing participants to answer in a way that facilitated them to relate their responses to the environment that they were currently operating in. The nature of the data gathered would clearly have been changed by undertaking the same study using face-to-face or telephone-based interviewing. However, it would also have been changed by using other online technologies (chat rooms, video-conferencing software, discussion boards etc.). The rest of this chapter explores some of the options that are available to the online qualitative researcher in more detail, and considers how to use them most effectively in undertaking research projects.

Understanding qualitative methods

As elsewhere in this book, this chapter focuses on the translation of social research methods (in this case interviews and focus groups) to the online environment. If you are not familiar with the use of such qualitative methods as interviews and focus groups, you may wish to consult one of the many general introductions that are available. For a general introduction to qualitative research methods, see Flick (Flick 2009a) or Berg (Berg 2008), or for a practical student guide to conducting qualitative research, see Silverman (Silverman 2009). For a more focused text on interviews, see Kvale and Brinkmann (Kvale and Brinkmann 2008) or King and Horrocks (King and Horrocks 2010), and for focus groups see Stewart et al. (Stewart, Shamdasani and Rook 2007) or Krueger and Casey (Krueger and Casey 2009).

While there are important methodological differences in the use of online interviews and focus groups, most of the differences are similar to the ones that researchers will be familiar with from onsite research. In this chapter, therefore, the distinction between interviews and focus groups is made only where the methodological issues intersect with the online environment.

As with the previous chapter, it is perhaps worth beginning with some basic definitions:

- Interviews involve an interaction between a researcher and a research participant for the purpose of gathering qualitative data. Interviews typically gather both factual and interpretative data, and can use a variety of different approaches (structured/unstructured, life history, thematic etc.).
- Group interviews use a similar approach to individual interviews but apply it to a group. It would be common for the group to comprise individuals with a shared characteristic or background. Data is derived from the group's answers to the questions, but also from their interactions with each other.
- Focus groups are a specialized form of group interview in which participants are asked to interact around a particular theme or set of issues. Participants are often selected to be representative of a particular population. Typically focus groups seek to reveal opinions, attitudes, beliefs and reactions rather than to establish facts.

When to use online methods for qualitative research?

As with all online research methods, the use of online interviews and focus groups has both advantages and disadvantages in relation to their onsite equivalents. Madge *et al.* note a number of advantages, such as savings in travel, cost and time, increased flexibility for both interviewer and interviewee, and some indications that participants may find certain types of disclosure easier in the online environment (Madge, O'Connor, Wellens, Hooley and Shaw 2006a; Joinson 2001). Some researchers have argued that the quality of data gathered from online focus groups compares favourably to that gathered in their onsite equivalents (Brüggen and Willems 2009). Others have argued that the use of online methods shifts the power balance between researcher and participants in the participants' favour, allowing them to exert more influence on the interview and to withdraw with less concern if they feel they no longer wish to proceed with the interview (Fielding 2010). When using text-based communication tools, the researcher is saved the usual time/money costs involved in the transcription of qualitative data.

However Madge *et al.* also note that there are considerable downsides, arguing that participants need a certain level of technical competence to participate, that they may be easily distracted by things in their environment, that there are issues with identity verification and, perhaps most challenging of all, the loss of most visual and contextual communications and clues (Madge, O'Connor, Wellens, Hooley and Shaw 2006a).

Online interviews and focus groups offer new opportunities to the researcher, but they also offer considerable challenges. As with all methodologies, the use of online interviews and focus groups needs to be carefully selected to ensure that the methodology is suited to the research questions being investigated and the population with which the research is being conducted. Online interviews and focus groups are clearly better suited to populations who are digitally literate and who have experience of using the environment in which you are going to conduct online research. So regular chat room users are likely to find participating in a text-based synchronous focus group technically undemanding, while individuals who come to synchronous chat for the first time are likely to find this more challenging.

However, even within these populations there is likely to be variation in the degree of comfort that different individuals feel in expressing themselves in different environments. Karchmer notes that some participants might be more effective speakers than writers but, as Meho responds, the reverse is also true (Karchmer 2001; Meho 2006). In the context of focus groups this issue may take on an additional dimension as groups can be dominated by those with the fastest thinking and typing speeds rather than those with the loudest voices.

When deciding whether to utilize an online interview or focus group it might be useful to consider the following issues:

- **Access:** Is it easy or possible for you to get physical access to the research participants? Conversely, do your participants have easy access to a computer and a reliable internet connection?
- **Technical ability:** Are your participants likely to be comfortable using computer-mediated communications for their discussions with you?

- **Research topic:** Is the topic that you are researching bound up with your participants' use of computers/the internet?
- **Environment:** Is there anything about your participant's environment that will make it difficult for them to participate in an online interview/focus group or to attend an onsite interview/focus group?
- **Sensitivity:** Are you likely to raise sensitive topics or risk causing distress to your participant? How will you deal with this depending on whether an onsite or online method is chosen?
- **Anonymity and confidentiality:** What is your approach to anonymity and confidentiality? How is this enabled or problematized by your decision to undertake the research online or onsite?
- **Data handling:** How will you manage the data that is gathered through your interview/focus group? Does conducting the interview online help to manage issues with the resources available for transcription etc?
- **Visual clues:** Are visual/body language/context clues likely to be important to the research that you are doing?

As ever, there are no strict right and wrong answers that can provide you with a definitive answer as to when to undertake something online and when to undertake it onsite. However, working through the questions above may provide researchers with some insights around what is the most appropriate way to proceed.

It is important to recognize that the online/onsite distinction is not always rigidly applied. Many researchers combine online and onsite methods for a variety of purposes. Turney and Pocknee conducted research on attitudes to paternity testing and stem cell research (Turney and Pocknee 2005). They used conventional focus groups to gain insights into public attitudes, but then used asynchronous online focus groups to follow this up with targeted groups (fathers, mothers and people with Parkinson's disease and spinal cord injuries).

Choosing tools for online interviewing and focus groups

Making decisions about which tools to use is important when undertaking all online research. However, the discussion in the previous chapter about which tools to use for online surveys is essentially a technical question about matching the functionality of tools to the needs of a particular research project. As the James and Busher case-studies have already shown, in the case of online interviews and focus groups the technology and methodology are closely connected. The choice of tool is likely to exert considerable influence on the kind of interactions that the researcher is able to have with participants, and the kinds of data that it is possible to gather.

Undertaking qualitative social research is usually about creating a specialized form of communication between researchers and research participants. Much has been written about the nature of this communication; however, at root it is a form of communication like any other that requires information and meaning to be able to flow in at least two directions. Communication is something that internet technologies have developed to do in a vast number of different ways. Individuals and groups communicate online using email, SMS, chat rooms, discussion boards, blogs, social networking software, video-conferencing software and an ever growing number of other applications. Many of these can be re-purposed for use in social research relatively easily. Indeed, many offer functionality that ideally suits them for use in social research, such as production of transcripts of conversations, or opportunities to include or exclude participants from particular discussions.

Given this explosion of communication technologies, the researcher may feel faced with an over-abundance of tools. Furthermore, online communicative technologies have not just provided alternatives to existing forms of communication, they have also created new forms of communication and this raises further questions for the researcher. An example of a new form of communication is provided by Flickr, the online photo-sharing website. Users of this site post pictures, tag them with keywords, associate them with groups and entitle them. Other users then have the option to comment on those photos, add them to their own galleries and share them via other social media. All of these interactions offer the users ways of communicating meaning to each other. Whether a communication tool like Flickr will be used to conduct something along the lines of an interview or focus group remains to be seen, but the point is that online technologies open up both new ways to do established things and the possibility of doing new things. Researchers may wish to consider both of these possibilities as they design their methodologies. Some of these issues are picked up further in chapters 6 and 8.

Broadly, it might be possible to represent a typology of different tools for online qualitative research along two axes. On one axis it would be possible to distinguish between the time over which the interview takes place. Does it take place asynchronously over a period of time like the Busher and James email interviews? Alternatively, does it take place synchronously with interviewer and participant engaged at the same time? A second axis might be used to represent whether the interview is conducted principally in text or whether it utilizes multi-media tools to provide images, audio, video or any other kind of experience such as 3D gaming environments. This kind of conceptualization might give us a typology as follows:

Table 5.1 A typology of online interviewing techniques

Asychronous text-based methods Email Discussion boards SMS	**Asychronous multi-media methods** Photo and text combinations Video blogs and responses
Synchronous text-based methods Chat rooms Messenger service	**Synchronous multi-media methods** Video- and audio-conferencing

Synchronous or asynchronous?

If researchers are seeking to transfer existing methodologies online, it is likely that they will initially gravitate towards synchronous methods. The opportunity to conduct the interview in real time has the potential to create something that borrows from many of the techniques and methodological approaches associated with face-to-face interviewing or focus groups. Stewart and Williams argue that, by allowing participants and researchers to interact concurrently, an atmosphere is created that allows discussion to flourish and which mirrors in many ways the kinds of interactions that take place in face-to-face social research (Stewart and Williams 2005: 405).

Hinchcliffe and Gavin also found that (text-based) online synchronous interviewing was convenient and popular with the university students who were the participants in their study (Hinchcliffe and Gavin 2009). Similarly, Bullard and O'Brien in their study of 'info-savvy' web-designers found that synchronous online interviewing presented few obstacles to communication (Bullard and O'Brien 2011). However, it is clear that online synchronous interviews and focus groups have been used most extensively with participants who are already familiar with synchronous communication channels or who at least have high levels of digital literacy, such as Lang and Hughes' focus groups with peer-to-peer filesharers or O'Connor and Madge's research with 'cyberparents' (Lang and Hughes 2007; O'Connor and Madge 2003). How this methodological approach would transfer to those with lower levels of digital literacy is not clear.

Other researchers have found the kinds of interactions that take place during synchronous interviews and focus groups to be more problematic. Davis *et al.* found that participants performed in particular ways in online interviews in comparison to face-to-face interviews, and that online interviews were more prone to ambiguity of meaning (Davis, Bolding, Hart, Sherr and Elford 2004). Fox, Morris and Rumsey described the process of running an online focus group as 'fast, furious, and chaotic' (Fox, Morris and Rumsey 2007), and Mann and Stewart note that in the chaos of synchronous chat conversational turn-taking can become disrupted (Mann and Stewart 2000). Even in the case of one-to-one online interviews, conversational turn-taking can become problematized as researcher and participant struggle to maintain a structure in the face of delays and disruptions (Markham 2004). When engaged in synchronous text-based communication, people are able to speak when they choose and without regard or awareness that others are also speaking. This can add to the ambiguity of online interactions and can pose difficulties both in terms of managing and analysing online interviews and focus groups, as the researcher is frequently confronted with uncertainty about which question a participant is answering. While some of these issues are solved by moving to a video-conference approach, Fielding notes that turn-taking confusion remains as an issue (Fielding 2010).

If synchronous online interviews and focus groups promise, at least initially, the opportunity to transfer existing methods online, asynchronous methods require researchers to rethink the nature and purpose of interviews or focus groups. Kanayama argues that asynchronous methods create a new concept of time, which fosters new types of interactions with interview participants (Kanayama 2003). Meho reviewed the literature on email interviewing in 2006, and noted that some researchers reported conducting email interviews over many months with sometimes more than thirty email exchanges being made. This kind of extended time period means that the kind of data collected is potentially very different from that collected in a single synchronous encounter, and this in turn opens up both opportunities (for example, longitudinal data) and challenges (such as how much does the respondent change their perspective over the course of a six month interview?).

Gaiser argues that in the case of online focus groups there are considerable advantages to an asynchronous approach, as it is likely to be more technically straightforward and offer a familiar experience for the user that is similar to email (Gaiser 2008). Deggs, Grover and Kacirek justify their decision to use asynchronous focus groups because of the difficulty of co-ordinating their participants (busy part-time graduate students) to all participate at the same time (Deggs, Grover and Kacirek 2010).

However, Gaiser also notes that asynchronous focus groups present challenges for the moderator in maintaining control and direction. Furthermore Deggs, Grover and Kacirek note that maintaining participation in their focus group over an extended period of time was challenging, with participation rates steadily dropping throughout the life of the focus group (six weeks). They suggest that there would be value in reducing the length of time over which the asynchronous focus group ran in order to maintain a higher level of participation. They also argue that the researcher needs to remain closely involved with the focus group to encourage participants and pose additional questions. However, the researcher also needs to guard against becoming the loudest voice in the online space and to allow the participant-to-participant dynamics of the focus group to unfold.

O'Connor et al. suggest that the format and design of an asynchronous interview is also vital (O'Connor, Madge, Shaw and Wellens 2008). The email interviewer must think carefully about how many questions are initially sent out, so as not to overwhelm the interviewee. The question order and delivery are also important, as is the approach to introduce the interview. O'Connor et al. also express concern that the additional time offered by asynchronous methods to think and re-edit responses could lead to a 'socially desirable' response rather than a more spontaneous personal response.

Text-based or multi-media

Text-based tools are attractive to the researcher as they avoid the need for expensive and time-consuming transcription. They offer a number of other advantages too, such as allowing interviewers and participants to avoid potential communication difficulties related to disabilities such as hearing impairment (Hinchcliffe and Gavin 2009) or concerns about personal appearance (Fox, Morris and Rumsey 2007). Oringderff also argues that text-based online environments can offer social equalization as they offer actual or perceived anonymity, and offer both participants and interviewers fewer clues about socio-economic status, ethnicity, gender, nationality and disability (Oringderff 2004).

The core limitation to the use of text-based tools is the ability of the researcher and participant to type at an appropriate speed. These issues are considerably sharper in relation to synchronous methods, but do not vanish altogether in asynchronous environments.

Regardless of how effective interviewers and participants are in expressing themselves in text, text-based environments still offer very different forms of communication from a conventional face-to-face interview. Most obvious is the loss of conventional verbal clues. Subtleties like the nod of a head, making eye-contact or a gesture towards a particular participant are key to the way that researchers conduct face-to-face research, but disappear altogether in the online environment. The lack of these various clues brings with it the possibility of misinterpretation of questions or responses, and researchers often find a need to seek additional clarification or reassurance (Meho 2006). Meho argues that in some cases some of these lost verbal clues are compensated for through the use of emoticons and text-speak acronyms such as LOL (laughing out loud) or ROFL (rolling on the floor laughing). Conventions of this kind clearly have cultural associations that mean that they are unlikely to be employed by all participants.

Video-conferencing provides an alternative (and far less commonly utilized) tool for conducting online interviews. Sedgwick and Spiers utilized the tool to investigate the experience of rurally dispersed nursing students (Sedgwick and Spiers 2009). Their participants were familiar with the use of video-conferencing for other purposes (training, meetings etc.) and the technology was well supported in the locations where the students were based. Video-conference was preferred over audio-based approaches (such a telephone interviews) because it was believed that it would preserve more of the non-verbal and verbal signifiers of meaning, and thus would allow the researcher to capture more subtle data (although this was in part dependent on the high bandwidth/high-quality video approach that was possible within the context that Sedgwick and Spiers were researching). Bertrand & Bourdeau also argue that video-conference software offers richer data by enabling the researcher to observe, record and analyse the movement of the individual's body and face (Bertrand and Bourdeau 2010).

Sedgwick and Spiers reported that participants were happy with the use of video-conferencing for interviews. As with text-based interactions it is likely that some participants are able to utilize the technological environment more successfully than others. Fielding found that his participants in video-conference interviews and focus groups were diverse, and that 'some played to the camera; others had stage fright and showed second thoughts about their images being broadcast' (Fielding 2010). Sedgwick and Spiers also note that although it comes close, the use of video-conferencing remains a different kind of interaction to face-to-face interviewing. It is not possible, for example, to offer a distressed participant a tissue via video-conferencing software and, as Fielding notes, even when video quality is high, establishing genuine eye-contact remains extremely difficult.

Other issues in selecting tools

There is also a range of other issues that researchers may wish to keep in mind when selecting tools for online interviews and focus groups. The following questions are designed to help researchers to think some of these issues through:

- How easy is the tool to use, and is it familiar or unfamiliar to the researcher and the participants? A tool in common usage (such as email) is likely to present participants with fewer problems, but will also carry some cultural baggage associated with the way in which that tool is usually used.
- Does the tool carry or convey a particular institution or organization through branding, URL or any other means? Online spaces convey meaning to participants and so, for example, the use of a higher education institution's Virtual Learning Environment (VLE) will posi-

tion the focus group or interview within a different kind of context from something based in Facebook.

- How is data recorded, saved and managed? It is essential to work out how you are going to record your data before you start any research. Many tools now offer the opportunity to record sessions. However, if this is not available then some creativity may be required. (Sedgwick and Spiers combined a tape recorder with their video-conference interviews to enable them to produce a transcript.)
- How are confidentiality and anonymity ensured/protected? Researchers should investigate what data is publically available (perhaps through profiles that are generated as part of account creation) and what is collected by the tool that is being used (for example, are participants' IP addresses recorded?). Deggs, Grover and Kacirek recommend that a system is used that allows participants to generate a new username and password for the purpose of the research if they choose to do so (Deggs, Grover and Kacirek 2010).
- What are the financial and other resource issues associated with the tool for researcher and participants? Selection of particular software or tools may involve real costs (such as subscription charges) or necessitate the researchers and participants installing software or downloading plug-ins in order that they can interact. These may limit participants' ability to engage if they are unwilling or unable to add software to their browser or desktop.

It is also important that researchers pilot the use of any new tool before committing to its use for an entire study.

Managing online interviews and focus groups

Many of the challenges associated with managing online interviews and focus groups relate to the disembodiment of the researcher. This chapter has already discussed the challenges associated with the disembodying of the participant in terms of the loss of data experienced by the researcher. However, interviews and focus groups are inter-personal interactions, and as such are highly reliant on language, visual cues, tone and other communicative subtleties. The move into online environments removes many of these cues and reframes others. Researchers therefore have to think about how they are going to manage the social, relational and logistical issues in undertaking qualitative research whilst online.

Sampling and recruitment

Many of the challenges of disembodiment are first encountered during the initial approach to potential participants. However, it is also worth noting that many of the challenges associated with sampling and recruitment in relation to online interviews and focus groups are closely related to those experienced by onsite researchers. Rather than rehearse a more general discussion about sampling and recruitment in qualitative research, researchers may wish to consult MacDougall and Fudge, Ritchie and Lewis or Flick (MacDougall and Fudge 2001; Ritchie and Lewis 2003; Flick 2009b).

Much of the discussion around sampling in chapter 4 is also relevant in the context of online interviews and focus groups. It may be worth reviewing that chapter's discussion around issues such as identity verification, understanding the demographics of the population, and engaging participants and sustaining engagement. In essence, the question is whether the use of online methods excludes any individuals or groups or makes anyone less (or more) likely to wish to participate. Many online researchers (Fox, Morris and Rumsey 2007) use the internet as a core element of their strategy to engage and recruit participants, and this is likely to have an impact on the nature of the sample that is recruited. However, it also offers opportunities to recruit participants quickly and in a way that is not dependent on personal access to participants or traditional gatekeepers. Nevertheless, as Hamilton and Bowers point out, website managers and discussion group moderators effectively become a new type of gatekeeper to research populations (Hamilton and Bowers 2006).

Although many of the issues around sampling for quantitative research remain, qualitative researchers are likely to find these less limiting. Interviews and focus groups do not generally seek to be representative, but rather to access the experiences and perspectives of participants to provide richer and deeper understandings of research issues. However, qualitative researchers do need to be careful in the construction of their sample frame and endeavour to avoid recruitment bias. Hamilton and Bowers note that 'if sampling is restrictive in a dimension important to the research question, then the results will not be representative of the experience in question' (Hamilton and Bowers 2006: 824). Salmons argues that researchers should be particularly attentive to whatever information is available (from academic literature, the census or other data sources) about the participants' access to technology and their digital literacy during the creation of the sample frame (Salmons 2009).

A key aspect of the recruitment process is the gathering of consent from participants. The approach that is taken onsite (information sheets, consent forms, verbal explanation and signature) is problematized considerably by the movement online. Some researchers have argued that there is value in retaining hard copy consent-form processes even if the research is actually being conducted online (Hamilton and Bowers, 2006). However, this seems increasingly archaic in a world in which ever more transactions are conducted entirely online. Therefore it is important in consent processes that participants have had the opportunity to become informed about the research and their role within it, to ask questions and clarify concerns, and that this process is recordable and evidencable in some way. Whether it takes the character of an online form, emailing a Word document or recording a synchronous discussion is less important than the fact that the process takes place.

Building rapport

The building of rapport could be conceptualized as involving three inter-related elements: the researcher; the participants; the cultural environment. How the researcher behaves by being open, friendly, flexible and empathetic clearly forms an important part of the process of rapport building. However, the participants also influence how this process plays out and their attitudes, assumptions and experiences will influence this. Finally, the nature of the online environment in which the research is being conducted will influence the success or otherwise that researchers and participants have in striking up rapport.

Conventional qualitative methodologies emphasise the building of rapport as a key component of undertaking research. Madge *et al.* note that traditional techniques employed by the researcher (dressing appropriately, smiling, making eye-contact) have to be abandoned or re-imagined in the context of online interviews and focus groups (Madge, O'Connor, Wellens, Hooley and Shaw 2006b). Orgad notes that many of these physical signifiers are replaced with alternative online signifiers, such as the interviewer's email address which convey meaning and therefore help or hinder the building of rapport (Orgad 2005).

Recognizing the variety of ways in which meaning is signified, and trust built online, offers researchers opportunities to build rapport. Kivits consciously disclosed personal information to participants as part of this rapport building (Kivits 2005), while O'Connor and Madge provided participants with access to a website with photos and personal information about them to increase their trustworthiness (O'Connor and Madge 2001). Openness of this kind offers one strategy through which some of the limitations of web-based communications can be offset. If participants are to feel comfortable with a researcher, the researcher needs to establish their credentials as a trustworthy human being. In conventional research settings much of this work is done through the verbal and non-verbal signifiers that are employed with varying degrees of consciousness by researchers. Without these signifiers alternatives have to be found that can achieve the same result.

However, researchers also have to recognize that it is not just their actions that can influence the development of rapport. Participants may seek to interact in different ways from the researcher, perhaps pursuing their own agendas or enacting the communication in ways that confound the researcher's notions of rapport (for example, more formal/less formal). When the researcher is attempting to build rapport with a group rather than an individual these issues become more complex still. Oringderff argues that in online focus groups individuals may experience more freedom with a corresponding reduction in the amount of discretion and tact (Oringderff 2004). This kind of behaviour has the potential to undermine the successful functioning of the group and should probably be consciously addressed by the researcher. Similarly, Oringderff notes that in certain groups participants may cease interacting as a group and instead form smaller groups or 'pair friendships'.

Finally it is also important to note and consider the opportunities for rapport building that are offered by the environment within which the interview/focus group is taking place. For example, does the environment enable the sharing of profile photos amongst participants? Does it offer features that enable participants to convey emotions or ideas in paralinguistic ways, such as a button for 'I'm confused'? Does the environment allow you to formalize turn-taking or send messages to a single participant rather than the whole group? Researchers are advised to experiment with the functionality of the environment to explore these kinds of possibilities and consider how they might be employed in the building of rapport and the management of the group.

Dealing with problems

Interviews and focus groups depend on the establishment of a workable contract between researchers and participants. Much of this is about building rapport and creating an atmosphere in which participants want to engage in the research. However, once engaged the researcher still has to manage carefully the interview/focus group to ensure that it proceeds in a way that is useful. Questions and other researcher inputs are designed to shape discussions in ways that illuminate the research questions or themes. However, the agenda of the research will rarely match exactly that of the participant.

Typically researchers have a range of tools to help to manage the environment and conduct of the research. Particular locations might be chosen, furniture organized into particular configurations, the researcher might choose to wear particular clothes, to encourage turn-taking by the use of eye-contact and so on. All of these different and subtle signals help to convey to the research participant the nature of the encounter, expected behaviour and how to participate. When the interview is moved online many of these strategies need to be rethought.

The following strategies might be employed to help researchers manage online interviews and focus groups:

- **Contracting:** beginning interviews with a discussion about the purpose and format of the interview to help set some ground rules.
- **Netiquette:** attending to the online etiquette (netiquette) that is commonly in use by research participants. It may be useful to remind people if you feel someone has breached netiquette, for example by flaming (insulting) someone else.
- **Pre-prepared responses:** it can be useful to have some prepared sections of text ready, given the speed with which (synchronous) online interviews and focus groups move. These could be concerned with providing stimulus to the discussion or with dealing with challenging behaviour by reminding people of agreed behaviours. The use

of pre-prepared text can allow researchers a little more time to read and respond to contributions.

- **Sending individual messages:** many discussion tools allow the researcher to message individual participants during a group discussion. This can be useful to clarify meaning, check on whether participants are OK and address problem behaviours.

An additional problem for researchers in online environments is dealing with participants who just vanish. Participants may leave because they have experienced technical problems, because they get bored, are committed elsewhere or because they object to the actions of the researcher or another participant. For researchers this can be disconcerting, and they may wish to follow up with participants by email or phone to further explore the reasons for their departure.

Analysis

In many ways, the analysis of data collected during online research is the same as the analysis of other kinds of qualitative data. A big advantage is the default production of full text transcripts or video recordings of the interview. However, it is also important to remember that the medium shapes the nature of the interaction and the kinds of data that are collected. As Fielding argues, 'No research technology, from pen and paper through to AG[access grid], is a neutral "carrier" to the field. All research technologies reconfigure the field' (Fielding 2010). The nature of the data being gathered therefore has a relationship to the way in which it is gathered, and the analysis needs to reflect on this and consider its implications.

Depending on the tools and methodologies employed by the researcher, the kinds of data that have been generated will vary. Furthermore, the epistemological and methodological approach will shape the researcher's analytical approach to the material that they have gathered. However, there are a number of issues that researchers might wish to attend to as they analyse the material that they have gathered:

- **Inaccuracies:** online interview transcripts are typically littered with typing errors and spelling mistakes, as well as the use of text speak and paralinguistic signifiers (LOL, :-> etc). The researcher needs to consider how much of the analysis needs to explore and reflect the mode of expression.

- **Spatiality:** how far should the analysis take account of the physical location and life context from which data have been generated? Orgad argues that combinations of online and onsite data can enrich the analysis and help researchers to understand what online data is saying (Orgad 2009).
- **Conversational flow:** how does the altered nature of conversational flow (for example, less sequential in synchronous, slow genesis in asynchronous) alter both the nature of the data collected and the analysis?
- **Silence:** how should the analysis attend to silence and pauses in transcript data? Often transcripts will be time-coded in a way that makes it easy to examine pauses, but they may not mean the same thing socially as they might in a face-to-face interview.

In summary

Online qualitative research remains a relatively new area in which methodological approaches are still becoming established. The rapid development of new forms of communication technology complicates this still further. As researchers begin to establish methodological processes for email, discussion boards or chat rooms, new technologies are developed (for example, social networking software and smart phones) that necessitate the recontextualising of methodologies in both technical and socio-cultural terms. Given this context of change and flux, it is unlikely that online interviews and focus groups will ever reach a point where methodology is stable. Researchers therefore need to be reflexive in their methodologies and learn from their experience, the experience of others (including participants), and from the changing social and technical environment around them.

Further reading

Online interviews and focus groups have not been as extensively discussed as online surveys. *Online Interviewing* (James and Busher 2009) provides an overview of key methodological issues and is particularly strong on asynchronous interviewing. *Online Interviews in Real Time* (Salmons 2009) provides a practical approach to synchronous interviewing.

6 Online ethnographies

The movement of ethnographic approaches online presents some challenging methodological and ethical questions. Sometimes referred to as netnographies (Kozinets 2010) or virtual ethnographies (Hine 2000), this research method explores how humans live and interact online through a wide range of different research strategies. Hine argues that ethnographic researchers start from the perspective of questioning what is taken for granted and seeking to analyse and contextualize 'the way things are' (Hine 2000: 8). In relation to the internet this means that researchers challenge the notion that the internet is the product of the features of its technology, and explore how it is constructed by the way in which people inhabit, utilize and actively make it.

This interaction between social and technological conceptions of the internet forms a key context within which online ethnographies are pursued. Like other online researchers, online ethnographers need to answer a range of methodological questions such as how to gain access to the population that is being researched, how research participants are engaged, encountered and related to, and what is the blend of observation and participation being used. However, many of the strategies that served ethnographic researchers in the exploration of geographically situated communities need to be reframed. Furthermore, the diffuse, networked nature of online relationships can make communities difficult to identify, delimit and analyse. On the other hand, the technological and social practices of the internet mean that personal and community data are more open and easier to access than ever before. People tend to exhibit heightened self-disclosure when engaging in computer-mediated communications (Joinson 2005). For ethnographic researchers used to a careful process of building trust and mutual respect as part of data-gathering strategies, this self-disclosure and access to vast amounts of naturally occurring data can raise some uncomfortable possibilities.

This chapter examines the practice of online ethnographers, and looks at how far these practices are simply the translation of offline techniques and how far they represent a reimagining of ethnographies in a new context. The chapter asks whether data mining of online populations can be justified, and whether this kind of analysis of online material can be described as an ethnographic study. Furthermore, it examines how the growth of social tools to support community interactions and user generation of content can be utilized by the online ethnographer.

The chapter begins by presenting a case-study exemplar, before moving on to identify key texts and lessons from the literature. The advantages and disadvantages of the method are then explored, and strategies for overcoming challenges identified.

case study

Undertaking fieldwork inside and outside of World of Warcraft

Ethnographic research can take a wide range of forms, and so it is difficult to offer a case-study that is in any way typical. The diversity of different kinds of ethnography is one of the most striking things about the research that has been published within this area. Before beginning the main case-study it is perhaps worth briefly sketching a couple of other mini case-studies which demonstrate the range of different approaches to online ethnography or fieldwork. Nelson and Otnes explored cross-cultural weddings through an examination of online wedding messages boards (Nelson and Otnes 2005). The researchers archived about 400 posts from three separate wedding message boards, and analysed and coded the posts as the basis of their study. The posts covered sixteen countries and one year. Research was primarily observational, although researchers did participate in the message board conversations to some extent.

A very different approach to data collection can be seen in Fields and Kafai who investigated young people's participation in an educational virtual world (Fields and Kafai 2009). Where Nelson and Otnes sought breadth, Fields and Kafai sought depth, focusing the study on twenty-one young people who attended an after-school club where the game was played. Their study utilized a wide range of data collection techniques, piling up data of various kinds to form an immersive 'thick' description of the experience of the young people.

Data collection approaches included fieldnotes, onsite observations of the club in action, video capture of the club, interviews, recordings of the game play and logfile data provided by the owners of the gaming site (with the young people's consent). Fields and Kafai's study immediately throws up two crucial issues that ethnographic researchers have to face. Firstly, the level of surveillance that was undertaken clearly requires careful negotiation and ethical consideration by the researcher. Secondly, it highlights how the vast amount, and diversity, of data that is generated by a relatively small number of participants can pose considerable analytical challenges.

Many of the issues raised by Fields and Kafai are also explored in Bonnie Nardi's work on World of Warcraft (WoW) (Nardi, Ly and Harris 2007; Nardi and Harris 2006). WoW is a Massively Multi-player Online Game (MMOG) in which players interact within a highly complex environment based on the fantasy genre. The work of Nardi *et al.* explores issues around collaboration, social interaction and social learning within the gaming environment. They situate their work within the tradition of participatory and immersive ethnographic fieldwork. Putting this simply, it means that they play the game as well as, and as part of, studying it.

Nardi *et al.*'s involvement with WoW is long-term and regular, and their understanding of the environment is grounded in this experience. Their ethnographic fieldwork is therefore based on reflections on the experience of playing, on observation and on interactions with other players within the WoW environment. They then supplement this with a number of interviews conducted outside the WoW environment (a mixture of online and face-to-face interactions).

The work of Nardi *et al.* raises a number of interesting methodological issues. Their studies demonstrate the complex interactions between online and offline social networks. In some ways, the WoW studies seem to connect to an older ethnographic tradition in which the researcher travels to an unfamiliar culture, participating in life there and building up an ethnographic narrative of the place/ culture. However, Nardi *et al.*'s work shows that WoW networks frequently comprise individuals playing in the same room, belonging to the same family or closely connected in other ways not related to WoW. Observational research that treats online environments as contained communities runs the risk of missing some of this complexity. Nardi *et al.*'s decision to participate in WoW, but also to step outside it, clearly led to the creation of a different kind of ethnography that was centred online but not wholly constrained by the online environment.

The above case-studies demonstrate some of the complexities that ethnographic researchers are likely to need to work through. Questions about the nature of online spaces and their intersection with onsite spaces run to the heart of online ethnographic approaches. These issues are discussed further throughout this chapter.

Ethnographic methods

Chapters 4 and 5 concentrated on particular research strategies (surveys, interviews and focus groups). However, online ethnographies do not provide a direct equivalent to these approaches. Ethnographic methods are eclectic and utilize a wide range of different research strategies. Many ethnographic researchers utilize surveys, interviews and focus groups amongst a wide range of other methods. In onsite research we might expect ethnography to make use of one or more of the following research strategies:

- Participant observation, especially seeking to notice things like patterns, common behaviours and rituals. Participant observation also seeks to notice the gaps between what people say and what they do. Sometimes some of this observation might be recorded using photos, videos, research diaries and other means.
- Interviews, including group interviews and focus groups.
- Surveys to gather both quantitative and qualitative data.
- Network analysis (such as observing and recording the relationships that exist within a community or a family).
- Topographic observation and analysis.
- Examination of documents and written and print culture.
- Material culture observation and analysis.
- Historical analysis.
- Data analysis.

Ethnographic research is defined, not by the use of a particular research strategy, but rather by an ethical and methodological approach to the research that is frequently holistic, embedded in the place where people are, and conducted over the long term.

Ethnography is a complex approach with a rich tradition of methodological discussion. Good starting points for investigating the approach can be found in Brewer and Hammersley and Atkinson (Brewer 2001; Hammersley and Atkinson 2007). It is important to recognize that ethnography describes both a research method (fieldwork) and a genre of writing. It is therefore extremely valuable to read a range of ethnographic writing in order to understand the approach. Good introductions would include Malinowski, Read, Fortun, Williamson and Dean (Malinowski 1922; Read 1980; Fortun 2001; Williamson 2004; Dean 2009), although this selection hardly does justice to the wide variety of ethnographic writing.

Many ethnographers would describe their method as being 'fieldwork', because it is the process of examining people and phenomena where they occur that is distinctive about ethnography. However, as Hine notes, 'the concept of the field site is brought into question. If culture and community are not self-evidently located in place, then neither is ethnography' (Hine 2000: 64). This problematicization of the idea of the 'field' is an essential issue for online ethnography, as has already been discussed in relation to the work of Nardi *et al.* in WoW. However, given this, the researcher may question how far it is possible to divide online ethnographies from other ethnographies. It would be possible to see distinctions between researching online communities and how geographical (or other) communities interact online. However, the distinction is rarely as clear-cut as this, and researchers are likely to find that they need to approach online ethnographies with a range of flexible methodological tools. In the literal sense no one lives online, and individuals remain in physical space whilst they interact online. As Garcia *et al.* argue, '"Virtual reality" is not a reality separate from other aspects of human action and experience, but rather a part of it'. So where should the ethnographer be whilst conducting fieldwork? (Garcia, Standlee Bechkoff and Cui 2009: 54.)

Orgad argues that 'capturing both sides of the screen' (triangulating) can increase the validity of interpretation of data (Orgad 2005). Fields and Kafai's study shows how this kind of multi-site and multi-method approach can be powerful (Fields and Kafai 2009). However, it is not always practical or relevant to research in this kind of intensive manner. Kozinets poses three questions for researchers in considering the blend that they might seek in relation to online or onsite ethnographies (Kozinets 2009: 66):

- How integrated or separate are the online and offline lives of the individuals and communities that are being studied?
- How important is the observation of offline behaviours? Kozinets gives the example of an online community in which people discuss their pets. In this case it might be important to observe how they interact with their pets as well as how they discuss this online.
- How important is it to be able to identify and verify the identity of community members?

The exact shape of the research methodology will depend on how the researcher answers these questions, on the research questions they are asking, on the resources available and on the level of access granted by participants in the research. All of these factors will influence the particular blend of research strategies that are used and help the researcher to balance the amount of activity that is online with alternatives such as face-to-face, telephone or postal data collection.

Choosing a fieldwork site

Traditional ethnography is often highly concerned with geographical space. Fieldwork practices often involve immersion in the life of the community being studied. However, online ethnography challenges some of these notions about what comprises a fieldwork site and necessitates the reinvention of ethnographic fieldwork practices.

One of the key methodological questions that online ethnographies need to address is where the boundaries are drawn in relation to the online community. This chapter has already discussed the issue of how far communities can be said to exist wholly online or offline. It is clearly possible to make arguments from a range of perspectives, but increasingly the distinction between online and offline communities is being blurred. Ellison, Steinfield and Lampe argue that the more recent generation of online community tools (such as Facebook) have a far greater relationship to existing (and often geographically proximate) social networks than the earlier communities described by Hine (2000) and the other early online ethnographers (Ellison, Steinfield and Lampe 2006).

In addition to the way in which online networks are overlaid with onsite relationships, they are also multi-modal (Markham 2004). Online interactions frequently take place across a wide range of different platforms with conversations being conducted across blogs, micro-blogs, social networking sites and other media. Drawing the boundaries for an ethnographic study is considerably more complex that deciding on an online or offline focus. Hine argues that 'technologies are not research sites in themselves and that it is a mistake to think that a given technological platform necessarily delivers a meaningfully bounded research site' (Hine 2005: 111). People are active in an ever increasing range of different kinds of environments. As discussed in chapter 5, these environments both replicate existing forms of communication and make new forms of communication possible. An incomplete list of the ways in which people interact and form networks of associations online might include some of the following:

- Audio/video sites.
- Blogs.
- Chat rooms.
- Forums (bulletin boards, discussion boards).
- Lists, listserves or email lists.
- Micro-blogs.
- Photograph sharing.
- Playspaces, sometimes referred to as MMOGS, MMORPGS, ARG, MUD and MOO (see Glossary).
- Presentation sharing.
- Social bookmarking.
- Social networking sites.
- Social news.
- Virtual worlds.
- Wikis.

Inevitably, this list will continue to grow and shift as technology, and cultural responses to it, develop. In some cases online communities may exist entirely contained within one or other of these sites, but increasingly communities exist, in the words of Weinberger, in 'small-pieces, loosely jointed' (Weinberger 2003). In other words web communities are frequently not confined to a single technological platform; nor is it easy to identify the boundaries of the communities in a straightforward way. Researchers can use search tools to identify communities for ethnographic research by finding out where particular issues are being discussed. Sometimes online communities and social media are poorly represented in conventional search tools and it may be useful to use tools like Google's

Blog search or Realtime search to access appropriate communities more quickly. Kozinets argues that communities that are identified as appropriate for ethnography should meet most of the following criteria (Kozinets 2009: 89):

- Relevant.
- Active.
- Interactive.
- Substantial.
- Heterogeneous.
- Data-rich.

Each of these different sites provides the ethnographic researcher with a range of different signifiers to observe and explore. Chapter 5 looked at how conducting research in a text-based environment differed from the use of multi-media environments. Ethnographic approaches are likely to encounter similar issues, but with still further complexity. Online spaces utilize a wide range of technologically based signifiers which are conveyed through audio, video, text, images, avatars and many more means. However, the way in which these elements are assembled is a question of technology (how the environment is set up) and culture (what the participants do to shape the environment). So an environment like Second Life offers participants particular technologies to enable interaction (avatars, text chat, etc.) but it also offers them the opportunity to shape the virtual topography and cultural milieu. Not only do ethnographers need to attend to all of these various factors, but they also need to be able to explore their creation historically and technically.

Furthermore, many online environments have further sub-divisions that allow the development of finer focuses. For example, in Carter's research on Cybercity, she was able to focus on a single neighbourhood within the environment (Carter 2005).

Gaining access

Once the focus for the study has been identified, the researcher is faced with the task of negotiating access. One of the challenges is that much personal and community data is freely available on the internet, so that the process of negotiating 'access' may become almost meaningless.

In many cases it would be possible for a researcher simply to harvest the conversations and interactions of online communities without the communities themselves being aware of it. However, Kozinets argues that online ethnographies should be participative and build on the ethical approaches associated with onsite ethnographic research (Kozinets 2009: 75). He makes the case passionately, arguing that 'if we want to write netnographies that can stand up to the standards of quality ethnography, filled with deep understanding and thick descriptions, then lurking, downloading data, and analysing while sitting on the sidelines are simply not options'. Hine also argues that researchers should recognize the value of participation, arguing that the 'shift from an analysis of passive discourse to being an active participant in its creation allows for a deeper sense of understanding of meaning creation' (Hine 2000: 23).

However, it is important to recognize the dangers and challenges of participatory approaches. Orgad reflected that 'it proved extremely difficult to strike a balance between being attentive and empathetic to informants on the one hand, while maintaining a distance and appropriate researcher-informant relationship on the other' (Orgad 2005: 56). Orgad goes on to describe her discomfort in receiving an email from a participant stating 'I just know we will be friends for life'. Participatory research by its nature blurs the boundaries between researcher and researched and makes the process of 'striking a balance' extremely difficult. Researchers are advised to think through this relationship carefully in methodological, ethical and personal terms before embarking on fieldwork, and to reflect on the approach as the situation develops. Clear boundaries and roles are important, but the complexity of human relationships encountered during participatory research has a habit of overwhelming them. These issues about the levels of participation and disclosure are picked up in this chapter's discussion of data collection. However, many of these issues are likely to receive particular scrutiny during ethical approval processes, as discussed in chapter 3.

How researchers approach online communities/networks/groups will depend on their methodological approach and their research aims. While it is difficult to generalize, the following ideas might be helpful in building trust and engagement:

- Take time to find out about the communities you are entering before you announce your project. This is likely to give you some clues as to what approach to take and how to avoid offending or confusing people.

- Be aware that attempts to enter communities and provision of information about research projects (however worthwhile) may be perceived as intrusion or spamming. This is particularly the case in communities that have been researched before, especially if that experience was not a good one.

- Consider whether you want to lurk (watch without participating) before you announce your presence and whether you will be collecting data whilst you lurk. Shoham used this strategy as part of gaining access to the chat room community he was researching (Shoham 2004). There may be ethical issues in lurking (especially if it is the sole method of data collection), but it is also likely to enable you to be able to judge the appropriate tone of an initial post.

- Enable (potential) participants to find out further information about your project and research aims – perhaps by directing them to a website or blog. Try to avoid deluging people with information at the initial point of contact, and use accessible language when you do provide them with information.

- Think about how much time/disclosure/engagement you are asking for when you first approach. Joinson notes that participants are more likely to be engaged if trust is first established through small interactions before a more substantial request is made (Joinson 2005: 28). He refers to this as the 'foot in the door' principle.

- Consider whether you bring gifts when you arrive. Do you want to provide participants with useful and interesting information that is relevant to their interests as well as explaining that you will be studying them for your interest.

Data collection

Once the researcher has negotiated access, they will be able to draw on a wide range of different data sources. There is a vast number of types of data that can inform online ethnographies, many of which draw on the visual methods tradition (Mason 2005; Knowles and Sweetman 2004; Banks 2001).

While it is possible to list the variety of forms in which you can find online data, Kozinets moves beyond this to conceptualize different kinds of data, as shown below (Kozinets 2009: 98).

Table 6.1 Koszinets' typology of online data

Archival data	What happened	Transcripts of interactions, recordings
Elicited data	What you were told	Interviews and direct interactions with participants
Fieldnote data	What you saw and what you made of it	Participant observation, reflection, *in situ* analysis

Archival data

Archival data in this context describes naturally occurring data that the researcher has collected through some means for the purpose of the study. Naturally occurring data can be scooped up and downloaded through an increasing number of techniques. Some researchers record data using screen shots or screen recorders, while text-based interactions can often be downloaded directly into databases using RSS feeds or other similar protocols. Through using these kinds of archiving techniques, researchers can access a range of personal and collective forms of conversation, disclosure and publication, such as blogs, micro-blogs, posts on social networking sites, message boards, chat rooms and many other kinds of online interaction.

The exclusive use of archival data can sometimes be controversial for ethnographers, and can be described in negative terms as data mining or data extraction. When Langer and Beckman downloaded 896 posts to a plastic surgery message board for analysis, without participant permission, they devoted space in their article to justifying their 'pragmatic perspective' on covert research (Langer & Beckman 2005). They argue that the ethical positions taken by Kozinets around informed consent are impractical and overly stringent for discourse that is taking place in open public forums (Kozinets 2002).

Much of the discussion about the use of archival data without permission hinges on how the status of open data on the web is perceived. Where data is publically available, some researchers might argue that there is no reason to treat it any differently from any other public media. Many bloggers are clearly and actively engaging with the public sphere, and researchers may feel happy with analysing their posts in the same way as a newspaper article might be examined. However, Shirky's conceptualization of the internet as a series of 'small worlds' can problematize this (Shirky 2009). Individuals are often publishing their thoughts for the benefit of their own small world or social circle, and may not have thought carefully about how this data might be reused and represented. Garcia backs up this concern by noting that across a range of studies participants say that they feel uncomfortable with covert researchers who do not reveal their identity or the reason for their engagement in the online space (Garcia 2009: 73).

The distinction between archival data and fieldnote data can often be fine. Because of the vast array of naturally occurring data produced by web users, the decision to record one thing and not another is essentially an analytic one. For example, a study that gains access to web statistics but does not undertake a content analysis of what is on those web pages is making an analytical decision about what is important (in this case where people went rather than what they said). In conventional ethnographic work, accessing such data would require the creation of fieldnotes, and would ideally entail a process of reflection and justification of what is being recorded on them.

Gathering archival data is clearly a more complex process than it initially appears. While technology increasingly facilitates the process of large-scale data mining, the researcher still has to navigate the ethical, methodological and analytic challenges of accessing naturally occurring data and using them to explore research themes or address research questions.

Elicited data

Elicited data describes the researcher's direct interactions with participants both within the research environment and outside it. Researchers will typically elicit data to help understand their observations and to enrich the understanding of archival data. So Carter describes using 'as many methods as I could to collect a wide variety of rich data. Therefore, as well as practising ethnography, I carried out other qualitative research methods including questionnaires and offline semi-structured interviews.

Towards the end of my research I also met four of my informants face-to-face (Carter 2005: 150).

Data could be elicited during participatory research, perhaps by asking for clarification about meaning in a discussion. Alternatively, data can be elicited using the kinds of strategies described in chapters 4 and 5. Many ethnographic research studies combine participant observation approaches with more formal types of elicitation. For example, Hammam combined participant observation with online interviews in his study of cybersex (Hammam 1997), Maulana and Eckhardt elicited data through interview and participant diaries, and combined this with participant observation in their study of the relationship between website and site visitors (Maulana and Eckhardt 2007), and Gatson and Zweerink undertook participant observation, synchronous and asynchronous interviews and online surveys in their study of a Buffy the Vampire Slayer fan message board (Gatson and Zweerink 2004).

Fieldnote data

The final kind of data that is gathered through ethnographies is what Kozinets refers to as fieldnote data (Kozinets 2009). As has already been discussed, the conventional practices of taking ethnographic fieldnotes are transformed by the move to the online environment as firstly the field and secondly the purpose of note taking are reshaped. The ability to record highly detailed archive data about what is being observed removes the core function of much fieldnote taking, namely to set down what is actually happening to provide a basis for analysis.

Given the availability of high-quality archival data, it is possible to see fieldnote data fulfilling two main functions. Firstly, the taking of fieldnotes allows for an initial stage of *in situ* analysis to take place. The purpose of taking notes is not to set down what is happening (which can be archived), but rather to begin the process of understanding why it is happening and making connections with other things that have happened elsewhere (observation). Secondly, the process of taking fieldnotes allows the researcher to set down their own experience and reflect on this experience (participation and reflection).

Williams argues that the process of observing and taking fieldnotes in online ethnographic research is less intrusive than in conventional field sites, as participants do not have to be distracted by the notebook or tape recorder whilst they are going about their business (Williams 2007). However, if combined with archiving strategies, the process of observation and recording of observation is different from the taking of conventional fieldnotes and can be seen as essentially a process of proto-analysis. Leander and Mckim argue that the researcher should be attentive to the issues of time and space as well as attending to the content of what is said (Leander and Mckim 2003). Why do people decide to carry on one conversation in Twitter and another in Facebook? What are the implications of this kind of online space decision, as well as the physical spatial decisions about where to access the online conversation from (home, school, laptop, phone etc.)?

Observation therefore seeks to notice what is said, but also to attend to the context within which it is said. This context becomes even more complex as textual forms of communication are combined with visual and audio ways of communicating. Williams describes the observation of graphical MMOGs – the importance of attending to things like avatar positioning and performance, appearance, dress, facial expression and use of gesture. In many MMOG-type environments, participants also have the opportunity to shape and interact with the topography of the environment, and so this also becomes a subject for observation and analysis. While it may be possible (and useful) to record many of these interactions as archive data and code them retrospectively, observation provides a useful strategy through which researchers can bring together analyses and develop theories.

Fieldnote data also seeks to record participation in terms of what the researcher did, what happened as a result, what was discovered and how the researcher experienced it. Participation is an important part of ethnographic methods. The experiential elements of participating in an online community (where do you do it, how do you feel, what devices do you use) are all part of an ethnographic study, and researchers should think about how they are going to capture some of this data. Techniques like reflective journals or blogging may provide good ways to capture and record some of this data.

Researchers also need to think carefully through their engagement and positioning within the online community. Orgad's point about striking a balance in researcher-informant relationships has already been discussed (Orgad 2005). Kozinets goes on to make a related point about the researcher's impact on the community as a whole rather than just an individual, stating 'a netnographer probably doesn't want to be leading the community, but she should not be invisible either' (Kozinets 2009: 96). Considering the approach to participation in online conversations is an essential part of developing the methodology for an ethnographic study. As with many methodological issues, there are no absolutes, but the development of a clear methodological approach is to be advised.

Wesch particularly emphasises the importance of participation and reflection in his work on YouTube (Wesch 2008). Wesch and his students explored the process of production of online videos as the entry route to online communities. While it would clearly be possible to study YouTube through a content analysis of the vast number of videos available on the site, Wesch's project asked researchers to become part of the community and to draw on the data of their own reflections, which in turn served as the subject matter for their participation in YouTube. The project's findings, around what he refers to as 'context collapse' in asynchronous video communication, became apparent through participation and would have been difficult to access through any other means. This form of participation draws on a tradition of auto-ethnography (Reed-Danahay 1997; Etherington 2004; Anderson 2006), and requires researchers to expose themselves in potentially uncomfortable ways.

While not all research may involve the level of participation of Wesch's work, there is clearly something to be learnt from the project's approach to reflexivity. Wesch's focus on YouTube allowed the experience of participant researchers to be captured almost from their entry point into the project. One area that researchers may wish to consider carefully is how their own emotional, social and intellectual journeys whilst undertaking ethnographic research can be captured and incorporated into the process of analysis and presentation.

Analysis and presentation of ethnographies

As the chapter so far has suggested, ethnographic research is multi-method and multi-modal. The process of bringing together a vast range of different and at times seemingly contradictory findings is a key skill of the ethnographer. While this challenge is not confined to the online researcher, it is true that participation in online networks can frequently lead to the proliferation of different data types and extremely rapid accumulation of datasets. Researchers may find themselves faced with mountains of text, pictures, audio, video, moving graphics and avatars, maps of networks and the outputs of a vast array of other ways in which individuals and collectives present and organize themselves online.

Scott Jones and Watt argue that the process of data analysis has been ignored in much methodological writing about ethnography (Scott Jones and Watt 2010: 157). They note that there are debates about how far such processes can usefully be systematized without losing the attention to the particular characteristics of ethnography. This chapter has already discussed many of the challenges that are associated with accumulation of large amounts of data through online research; however, it is also important not to forget that the online environment also offers a wide range of opportunities. The online researcher is likely to be able to find a wide range of tools which can aid ethnographic processes, such as the mapping of networks, the coding of qualitative data, searching through large datasets and so on. Some of these forms of computer-assisted representation and analysis of data are discussed further in chapter 8.

It would be possible to go into much more depth in discussing the process of analysis of online ethnographic data than can be done here. However, the following ideas may be useful in considering how best to develop analytical approaches:

- Consider your approach to the anonymity of data carefully. Search engines may be able to locate the source of any phrases that you have quoted. Carter also notes that the use of screen names does not protect anonymity, as users frequently employ the same screen name across a variety of different platforms and are often as recognizable by that name as by their given name (Carter 2005).
- Consider the approach to data archiving before embarking on research. While it can be tempting to consider the web as an online repository, it is important to recognize that there are limits to search and recall technologies – for example, Twitter archives hashtags for only around ten days. Are you going to use CAQDAS? If so, how are you going to get data into it?
- Consider what kind of coding approach you are going to use and how far this will be derived from your data as the project unfolds.
- Think about how open your data analysis is going to be. Will you consult with participants about the codes you are using or the findings that you identifying?

- Consider what audiences your findings will be disseminated to and in what forms. For example, it is common practice to use a blog to present project findings and reflections on the process to participants and other researchers (Chenail 2011).

In summary

Online ethnographic research offers a powerful approach for researchers seeking to explore human experience and interactions. While this chapter has focused on online ethnographies, it has also tried to recognize that the online/onsite distinction is becoming increasingly problematic. Researchers who use ethnographic methods will need to recognize the conceptual and organizational complexity of human relationships, and to develop approaches that engage with people online and onsite in a multi-method and multi-modal way. However, despite the complexity, there are also good reasons to be excited about the possibilities of online ethnographies. In particular, the vast expansion of naturally occurring online data alongside the increasing power of tools to search and interrogate it means that ethnographers are faced with a wealth of opportunities in interacting with online communities, networks and conversations.

Further reading

Virtual Ethnographies (Hine 2000) was one of the first works comprehensively to discuss online ethnographies, and is still worth reading. More recently *Netnography: Doing Ethnographic Research Online* (Kozinets 2009) provides a good overview of the major issues and approaches in the area, while 'Ethnographic Approaches to the Internet and Computer-Mediated Communication' offers an impressive and comprehensive literature review of the area (Garcia, Standlee Bechkoff and Cui 2009).

7 Online experiments

Researchers undertaking online experiments draw on a rich and long-standing methodological tradition that has been reworked and reformatted for a new environment. As with other online methods, a key question for the proponents of online experiments is how they compare to onsite experiments. In general, there is considerable evidence that suggests that the two return similar, if not identical, results and that online experiments offer a valuable tool which social science researchers may wish to utilize (Krantz and Dalal 2000).

Gosling *et al.* found that internet samples are relatively diverse with respect to gender, socio-economic status, geographic region and age; that findings were not adversely affected by non-serious or repeat responders; that findings are consistent with those from traditional methods (Gosling, Vazire, Srivastava and John 2004). Similarly, Meyerson and Tryon conducted a study to evaluate the psychometric equivalence of online research, and concluded that data gathered was reliable, valid and reasonably representative, as well as noting that the process of gathering data was cost effective and efficient (Meyerson and Tryon 2003). However, there are comparisons which have shown differences. Dandurand, Shultz and Onishi found that online participants were less accurate in their performance of tasks than lab-based participants (Dandurand, Shultz and Onishi 2008). Buchanan reviewed the literature on equivalence, and concluded that where there were (usually small) differences between the results of online and offline personality tests it was unclear as to why (Buchanan 2007). Alongside a call for further research, he speculates that the presentation of the instrument, the perception of online anonymity and computer anxiety may all play a role.

So although it is possible to see online experiments as equally as valid and reliable as lab-based experiments, this does not mean that they are identical. Online experiments require the development of an experimental approach that recognizes some of the particular challenges and opportunities that the environment offers. This chapter focuses on exploring when, where and how to most effectively use online experiments for social research.

Experimental methods in the social sciences

Experimental methods are well-established in areas such as psychology and behavioural economics, but can also be found in a range of different social science disciplines including sociology, political science and anthropology, as well as in inter-disciplinary areas, particularly those that cross over with technical or behavioural areas.

For further information about designing social science experiments, researchers may wish to consult *Laboratory Experiments in the Social Sciences* (Webster and Sell 2007) or *Social Experiments* (Orr 1998). Economists may also be interested in Levitt and List's article on experimental methods in economics (Levitt and List 2009), and psychologists in *Research Methods in Psychology* (Elmes, Kantowitz and Roediger 1999).

case study

Using Amazon Mechanical Turk

Suri and Watts undertook experimental research looking at the nature of co-operative behaviour (Suri and Watts 2011). Participants were recruited using an online labour market called Amazon Mechanical Turk (AMT) in exchange for micro-payments. This approach has been developed across a number of studies using AMT as a practical and effective method of recruitment. The typical interaction on AMT pays workers a small amount (less than $1) for conducting a short task. AMT recruits workers globally, although Rand notes that the majority are from either the US or India (Rand 2011). Rand also found that for the cost of less that $1 per person it was possible to collect data from over 1000 subjects in only one or two days. Paolacci, Chandler and Ipeirotis have also undertaken research using AMT, and argue that participants recruited from the site are 'at least as representative of the US population as traditional subject pools' (Paolacci, Chandler and Ipeirotis 2010: 411).

Following recruitment, Suri and Watts moved participants into a waiting room until they had collected a sufficient number to run the experiment. Their experiment dealt with co-operation, and required participants to interact synchronously. This in turn led to the need to corral them in a waiting room whilst a cohort was built. An initial design was tried which would have created groups of twenty-four; however, it was found that participants abandoned the waiting room before sufficient numbers had been recruited. An alternative approach was then developed in which four participants were recruited at a time for an initial task. Their details were then held to create a standing panel from which larger groups of participants could be recruited, with advance notice about the time of the experiment.

Suri and Watts conducted 113 experiments exploring how participants co-operated whilst taking part in an investment game. Participants were able to see the behaviour of a sub-set of the other participants, and asked to make investment decisions over the course of ten rounds. Participants had the choice to co-operate, not to co-operate, or to split their investments between a co-operative and non-co-operative position. Suri and Watts then used automated stooges to explore whether co-operative behaviour was contagious and to investigate other issues related to co-operation.

Suri and Watts argue that their research highlights the speed, flexibility and cost-effectiveness of web-based experiments over those conducted in physical labs. However, the process of conducting experiments online has the potential to offer researchers a range of opportunities beyond merely being cheap and convenient. For example, Suri and Watts were easily able to manipulate the experiment through the use of automated stooges without raising the suspicion of the participants. This would have been more expensive and complex to organize in a lab-based experiment. In their experiments in AMT, Paolacci, Chandler and Ipeirotis identify a similar benefit in the opportunity to reduce experimenter bias and participant crosstalk, noting that 'Mechanical Turk workers can complete experiments without interacting with experimenters, possibly without even knowing that they are in an experiment' (Paolacci, Chandler and Ipeirotis 2010: 415). Rand also notes that if you can gain access to the IP addresses of participants, it is possible to access information about them, their demographics and the areas from which they are accessing the internet (Rand 2011).

Some of these additional benefits of online experiments raise ethical questions that researchers may want to consider. In particular, issues around the appropriateness of payment for participation, particularly when combined with elements of deception or surveillance, merit consideration and may raise questions in some ethics approval processes. However, many of these issues are not specifically associated with online experiments, although in some cases they are made easier by the move online.

case study

Advantages and disadvantages of experimenting online

As with other online methods, online experiments have a number of advantages over onsite experiments. These are summarized by Reips (Reips 2002a) as:

- Faster speed.
- Lower cost.
- Greater external validity.
- The ability to experiment around the clock.
- High degree of automation of the experiment leading to low maintenance costs and limited experimenter effects.
- Wider samples.

Reips therefore argues that the internet is likely to become the setting of choice for many experiments.

Online experiments also suffer from many of the disadvantages already discussed for other online research methods. They can offer researchers less control over the environment in which the participant encounters the experiment, and the way in which the participant engages with it. So when Dandurand, Shultz and Onishi found that online participants completed their task less accurately than their lab-based participants, they attributed it to the possibility that online participants may have been simultaneously working on other things or have been distracted while completing the task (Dandurand, Shultz and Onishi 2008). There are also challenges around the verification of identity and the skewing of samples towards those who are digitally literate, or at least connected. The section on sampling in chapter 4 is worth looking at in relation to online experiments.

Table 7.1 (derived in part from Reips) examines some of the key disadvantages and challenges experienced in the use of online experiments, and suggests some ways in which these have been addressed.

Table 7.1 Addressing the challenges experienced in online experiments

Disadvantages/ Challenges	Solutions and examples
Possible multiple submissions	Multiple submissions can be avoided or controlled by collecting personal identification items, by checking internal consistency as well as date and time consistency of answers (Schmidt 1997), and by using techniques such as *sub-sampling*, *participant pools* or handing out *passwords* (Reips 1999; Reips 2000; Reips 2000). There is also evidence that multiple submissions are rare in web experiments (Reips 1997).
Researchers have less control over the experimental conditions	It is arguable that participants will be in conditions that are more typical than those encountered in a lab. Keller *et al.* noted that technical issues relating to the range of connection speeds, browsers and operating systems from which participants access experiments can reduce the reliability of an experiment in ways that are very difficult to track or adjust for (Keller, Gunasekharan, Mayo and Corley 2009: 1). However, some of these issues can be identified and avoided through testing, piloting and utilizing feedback. However it is also important to recognize that for some research questions lab-based experiments remain optimal.
Self-selection of participants and demographically limited samples	As has already been discussed in this book (chapters 1 and 4), the demographics of internet use are continuing to broaden. The sample can be broadened by recruiting participants from a range of sites. Much experimental work has relied on the use of undergraduates (Peterson 2001), so web -based samples can provide a broader sample.
Dropout and participant motivation	When and where people dropout whilst participating in online experiments can be used as a source of data about motivation and engagement. Dropout can be reduced by implementing a number of measures, such as promising immediate feedback, giving financial incentives and personalization (Frick, Bächtiger and Reips 2001).

Disadvantages/ Challenges	Solutions and examples
Reduced interaction with participants may lead to instructions being misunderstood.	This can be addressed to some extent by piloting the materials and by allowing participants the opportunity to feedback.

Many of the advantages and disadvantages associated with online experiments are closely related to those that have already been discussed in relation to other online methods. Furthermore, as Honing and Reips argue, there is considerable continuity in the challenges faced by the online researcher to those experienced by the onsite researcher (Honing and Reips 2008). For example, issues around identity verification or participant engagement are not new issues, even if they are reframed somewhat by the online environment. However, there are a number of features that are more specific to online experiments, which are worth exploring in more depth – in particular, the issues of automation, enhanced precision in observation, and the opportunity to undertake very large-scale experiments.

The ability to automate experimental procedures accounts for much of the reduction in costs by reducing the need to have an individual available to supervise participants and manage the experiments. However, Reips argues that this process of automation also increases the uniformity of the procedure and minimizes the impact of the researcher on participants (Reips 2002a). It is therefore arguable that the fact of automation can enhance the quality of the research as well as its efficiency.

The fact that all online experiments are mediated through a computer also offers an enhanced level of observation – for example, the ability to record reaction times without the participant being aware that they are being recorded (Kelso and Barchard 2005). Keller *et al.* also note the importance of this ability to record reaction time in some studies, and conclude that despite some of the technical difficulties in measuring reaction times, this is 'a very promising line of research' (Keller, Gunasekharan, Mayo and Corley 2009).

Perhaps most excitingly, online experiments open up the potential for very large studies. Salganik and Watts begin their article on the social dynamics of cultural markets with reference to Zelditch's question, 'Can you really study an army in the laboratory?' (Salganik and Watts 2009; Zelditch 1969). They note that entirely new kinds of experiments are now possible given the 'vast increase in computing power' and 'the almost limitless pool of participants now available via the internet'. It is now possible, they argue to move beyond the study of small groups towards the study of large groups, 'involving thousands, or even millions, of participants' (Salganik and Watts 2009: 440).

Deciding when an online experiment is appropriate

While there are good reasons to be positive about the value of online experiments, the online environment is clearly not appropriate for all research questions. Chapter 4 discussed this issue in relation to online surveys, and many of the limitations are similar in the case of online experiments. Researchers will want to consider whether the use of the internet is appropriate as they develop an approach to a research theme or question. Online experiments may not offer the most appropriate approach where identity verification, access to populations with low digital literacy or digital access, physical interaction with people or materials or a high level of control over the environment are important. However, as has already been argued, this is not to say that all of those issues are solved by conducting the research in a face-to-face environment.

An important area to consider during the development of methodologies is whether online and onsite experiments can be combined. Wiersma notes that there are a number of places where the distinction between online and onsite experiments becomes blurred, such as lab experiments preceded by an online survey, lab experiments validated over a number of sites, or the use of email as a stimulus for field experiments (Wiersma n.d). An example of an online/onsite combination is found in Burger, Charness and Lynham, who conducted related online and field experiments to explore students' self-control in relation to study behaviour (Burger, Charness and Lynham 2011). The field component enabled the researchers to examine students' actual behaviour, while the online element allowed a greater amount of control over the experience of the participants, a larger sample size and more rapid execution of the experiment. Taken together, the two experiments provided Burger, Charness and Lynham with more data which could inform their analysis.

Types of online experiment

As with other kinds of online research, there is a range of different types of online experiment. In a similar way to online interviews and focus groups, it might be possible to plot a matrix with synchronous and asynchronous on one axis and text-based and multi-media on the other (see chapter 5). Wiersma creates a similar typology, which examines the relationship between the technological and methodological approach that is taken in online experiments (see Table 7.2).

Table 7.2 Wiersma's typology of online experiments

	Lab	Field
Web-based	web	web-field
Virtual reality	virtual lab	virtual world

On one axis Wiersma counterposes web-based experiments with experiments that use virtual reality approaches. Web-based experiments use websites as their medium and draw on the tradition of lab-based experiments, often using similar elements (images, checkboxes and data fields). Virtual reality experiments provide an immersive environment where participants' behaviour is directly measured. Wiersma uses the examples of Second Life and World of Warcraft to describe his vision of virtual reality; however, it might be possible to broaden this definition out to include other kinds of interactive environment such as Suri and Watts' market simulations (Suri and Watts 2011).

Research which has looked at how people conduct themselves within virtual environments has often noted its utility for social research. For example, Kozlov and Johansen argue that virtual reality spaces offer experimenters an ideal space because they seem to offer a way to exercise a high level of experimental control, whilst offering a situation that is less contrived (Kozlov and Johansen 2010). They note that their participants exhibited similar behaviours in virtual reality environments to those that have been observed in lab- and field-based studies. However, they also note that the stronger the social presence of other participants in the virtual reality environment (the more they are perceived to be real human beings), the more participants treat them like human beings. The virtual reprise of the Milgram obedience experiments by Slater *et al.* also reported participants exhibiting similar behaviours in virtual environments to onsite environments (Slater, Antley, Davison, Swapp, Guger, Barker, Pistrang and Sanchez-Vives 2006).

Wiersma's other axis focuses on the methodological approach within which the experiment is situated. Is the experiment seeking to intervene in the actual online behaviour of individuals (the field), perhaps by bringing about a behaviour change in their use of a particular online tool or environment, or is it about bringing participants into a private or closed space (equivalent to a lab) in a way that does not interact with their daily lives and online activities?

Considering both the technical and methodological elements of an online experiment is key to designing the experiment. The nature of online research, and the methodological approaches that are used in it, are forged out of the conversations and compromises that are made between the technical possibilities and methodological approaches. This will be discussed further in the next section looking at designing online experiments.

Designing experiments

As has already been suggested, online experiments are not a methodology in themselves, but rather a particular mode through which experimental research can be conducted. Researchers are therefore advised to begin from their research questions or themes, and to develop a methodological approach in response to this. In some cases, this methodological consideration will lead towards an online approach, whilst in others it will lead to conventional lab or field approaches or to some kind of blend or hybrid.

For a general introduction to designing experiments in the social sciences, see Field and Hole or Webster and Sell (Field and Hole 2003; Webster and Sell 2007). More specific advice is also available for psychologists (Harris 2008), behavioural scientists (Open University 2006) and economists (Friedman and Sunder 1994; Hagel and Roth 1997). There are also a number of texts which provide specific advice in the design of online experiments such as Birnbaum, Reips and Gosling and Johnson (Birnbaum 2000; Reips 2007; Gosling and Johnson 2010). Some of these texts will be discussed in more detail in this section.

Once it has been determined that an online approach is appropriate, there are a number of key issues that researchers will need to work through.

These include:

- Experimental context.
- Considering what tools to use.
- Managing recruitment and avoiding dropout.

Experimental context

The context within which the experiment is conducted is a key decision that researchers need to make. The online space that is chosen enables or constrains both the functionality that the research is able to use (which will be covered in the next section on tools) and the social and cultural context within which the experiment is encountered. There is clearly a difference between completing an experiment within a university website, Facebook, the website of a supermarket or the website of a terrorist group. Each of these contexts is likely to impact on whether participants decide to participate, as well as the nature of their participation.

One useful way to conceptualize this would be to make the distinction between the online lab and the online field as potential sites for the experiment. So the study by Cosley *et al.* provided Wikipedia users with a stimulus (SuggestBot), and examined how user behaviour changed in response to exposure to SuggestBot (Cosley, Frankowski, Terveen and Riedl 2007). This kind of study might be described as a field experiment in comparison to Greiner, Jacobsen and Schmidt's 'virtual laboratory infrastructure for online economic experiments', which created a controlled environment for conducting economics experiments (Greiner, Jacobsen and Schmidt 2002).

Where experiments are conducted in the field, researchers need to attend to all of the ethical issues that they would in conventional field research. For example, if an experiment is conducted within Facebook, it may be being conducted in full view of participants' friends, colleagues and family, and an awareness of this public and open context needs to be built into the experiment design.

Contextual and environmental elements also have a role to play in online experiments within the lab paradigm. Kozlov and Johansen's decision to use a popular 'shoot 'em up' game as the site for their virtual lab may have created some contextual confusion for those participants already familiar with the environment in its usual form (Kozlov and Johansen 2010). As with physical environments, online environments are replete with factors and signifiers that may shape or influence participants' behaviours. Researchers therefore need to attend to these environmental factors during experimental design.

Considering what tools to use

The tools which are used to undertake online experiments are closely related to the issue of context. In many cases, the site that is chosen as the context will also form the experimental tools. So, for example, an experiment may offer a participant a virtual maze to explore (context), but the researcher will choose a site that enables the accurate recording of participants' behaviour, thus transforming the context into a research tool. In many cases the ability to manipulate the context to suit the needs of the online experiment will be a key tool required by the researcher. Konstan and Chen argue that the level of control offered by the website is crucial in deciding where to conduct the experiment, and that the best approach is to own the site (Konstan and Chen 2007).

This desire for a highly tailored and controllable experimental environment led Dandurand, Shultz and Onishi to craft their experiment using Java and Perl scripts (Dandurand, Shultz and Onishi 2008). Similarly, Kelso and Barchard discuss how 'easy' it is to hand-code web pages or use a What You See is What you Get (WYSIWYG) web-editor (Kelso and Barchard 2005). More recently, the growth of easy to use, web-based and often free tools has offered researchers a far wider range of opportunities to ensure that they have a high degree of control over the experiment. So while there are still going to be circumstances when researchers will want to build their own environment from scratch, as technology has moved on, the need to use scripting or mark-up languages has thankfully diminished.

Increasingly, it is possible to find highly configurable environments without needing to buy or purpose-build a site. Being a careful consumer of others' products is probably a more useful skill for the online experimenter than being a programmer. When creating online experiments, researchers are typically looking for a tool that offers some or all of the following functionality:

- Adaptable: the site needs to offer researchers sufficient flexibility and control to ensure that they can shape it to the experiments needs.

- Visible: researchers need to be able to see what goes on in their online environment.
- Enclosable: some experiments may require that researchers can control who has access to the environment and when people have access to it.
- Recordable: most research requires that what takes place in the online environment can be recorded in some way.
- Analysable: the online experiment needs to produce data in a format that it is possible for the researcher to analyse.

There are a number of purpose-built tools that researchers can use for online experiments. Reips offers a useful list on his 'tools for internet-based data collection' web page (Reips n.d). An alternative list is held by the Online Psychology Research website (Online Psychology Research UK 2011). It is difficult to recommend a particular tool, both because technology is dynamic and the tools continue to be born, develop and die in extremely rapid cycles, but also because every researcher and every experiment is different. The construction of methods needs to be done with an awareness of technological possibility, but not be driven by it.

Increasingly, researchers are finding that it is possible to adapt online tools that are designed for non-research purposes. So Koslov and Johansen's use of the game Half-Life 2 to provide a virtual reality environment for a replication of the Good Samaritan study by Darley and Batson provides one such example (Koslov and Johansen 2010; Darley and Batson, 1973). The case-study also showed how economists had used AMT for their research, and Schnoebelen and Kuperman also found it to be useful for linguistic research (Schnoebelen and Kuperman 2009). The growth of free tools is one of the phenomena of the contemporary web, and online researchers are likely to continue to find ways to use and re-purpose these for research. Tools like Google docs, various wikis and the range of tools available through the Digital Research Tools Wiki (DiRT) all merit a mention.

Managing recruitment and avoiding dropout

A key challenge in experimental design is creating an experiment that you will actually be able to get people to undertake and complete. The challenge of recruitment has already been discussed in chapters 4 and 5, and much of the learning can be transferred over to the area of online experiments. In particular, Madge *et al*'s checklist for online surveys can be easily re-purposed for online experiments (Madge, O'Connor, Wellens, Hooley and Shaw 2006).

Recruiting participants is challenging in all experimental studies. In some ways the online experiment is more challenging than its onsite equivalent, as engagement can be more difficult and the identification of a finite population from which to recruit is extremely challenging. On the other hand, the vast size of the online pool of participants offers some clear advantages. It is possible to advertise an online study from a wide range of places, such as Facebook, email lists, blogs, websites, discussion boards and so on. Reips argues that the quality of the participant pool can be enhanced by recruiting from multiple sites (Reips 2007).

There is also a range of web portals that exists specifically to recruit participants for online experiments. Some of these are listed below.

Table 7.3 Online portals for recruitment of participants

Krantz	Psychological research on the net	http://psych.hanover. edu/research/exponnet. html	A list of current online psychology experiments
Reips	Web Experiment List	http://www.wexlist.net	Intended to be the world's most comprehensive list of online experiments (both past and present)
Social Psychology Network	Online Social Psychology Studies	http://www. socialpsychology.org/ expts.htm	A list of online social psychology studies (including many online experiments)
Gardiner	Online Psychological Research	http://www. onlinepsychresearch. co.uk/	A list of online psychology experiments
Weijers and Richmond	The Inquisitive Mind	http://beta.in-mind.org/ online-research	A list of online studies

Most of the online recruitment portals are focused in the area of psychology. It is also unclear how effective they are in recruiting participants, and what kind of participants they tend to recruit. However, they provide a useful resource for researchers who are interested in examining other researchers' approaches, and who wish to experience an experiment from the perspective of a participant.

An alternative approach is to use some kind of payment or incentive to engage participants in an experiment. The case-study by Suri and Watts discussed the use of an online labour market and micro-payments as one way to recruit participants (Suri and Watts 2011). Alternatives include the use of participant pools and (paid or unpaid) online panels (Goritz 2007). While payment organized through an online labour market or a panel can incentivize participation and prevent drop-out, the evidence is more contested around the offer of lottery/prize draw type incentives. So while Frick, Bachtiger and Reips found that incentives did mitigate against drop-out, Goritz found no significant difference in relation to either recruitment or drop-out (Frick, Bachtiger and Reips 2001; Goritz 2006).

Closely allied to the issue of recruitment is that of dropout. An instructive example is found in Dandurand, Shultz and Onishi, who kept their online experiment open to all for 7.5 months (Dandurand, Shultz and Onishi 2008: 431). During that time the experiment received a total of 600 visitors. 62.7% of the 600 did not even start the experiment. An additional 16.3% were unable to complete the experiment due to technical reasons. Only 21% of those who looked at the online experiment started it and only 4.5% completed it. While it is difficult to generalize about dropout rates, it is clear that in most cases researchers can anticipate that a large number of those who start the experiment will not complete it.

Various approaches have been proposed to minimize or manage dropout. Reips recommends using warm-up tasks that are not part of the experiment in order to get dropout to happen before the experiment begins (Reips 2000). Other researchers have explored how the structure of an experiment can facilitate or limit dropout. O'Neil, Penrod and Bornstein found that placing requests for personal information at the start of the experiment heightened dropout, as did the use of over complex or poorly designed materials within the experiment (O'Neil, Penrod and Bornstein 2003). An alternative and ethically preferable approach is to think about the participants in a more positive way and to try to design, as Salganik and Watts claim they have done, 'experiments that are intrinsically rewarding for participants' (Salganik and Watts 2009: 461). Attending to the experience of the participant is an essential part of both experimental design and management. Kraut et al. note that 'researchers get less direct feedback from subjects than they do in other settings', and argue that this fact necessitates a greater attention to pre-testing and piloting of all elements of online experiments (Kraut, Olson, Banaji, Bruckman, Cohen and Couper 2004).

In summary

As with other online research methods, online experiments offer researchers considerable advantages. The decision to situate an experiment within the online environment is one that must be taken carefully and for sound methodological reasons. However, there is a wide range of advantages in terms of cost, time and improved quality. Perhaps even more exciting is the way in which online experiments open up the possibility for new kinds of studies, in terms of improving the quality of observations, the potential scale of experiments, and of course the ability to explore a range of topics directly related to the online environment.

As with all experiments, online experiments need to be designed carefully and to attend particularly to the nature of the online space within which the experiment is taking place. The idea of the online lab and the online field has been suggested as one way in which the nature of these online spaces can be conceptualized. How this is implemented through the use of a variety of purpose-built and adapted tools is also a critical question for the researcher to consider. Finally, this chapter has suggested that the online researcher should be highly aware of the experience of the participant. There are obviously key ethical reasons why this is important, but the reality of dropout in online experiments means that ensuring a positive experience is also essential for intensely practical reasons.

Further reading

There are a number of useful texts that can provide an introduction to the area of online experiments, in particular *Psychological Experiments on the Internet* (Birnbaum 2000). More recent additions to the field include *Oxford Handbook of Internet Psychology* (Joinson, McKenna, Postmes and Reips 2007), and *Advanced Methods for Conducting Online Behavioral Research* (Gosling and Johnson 2010).

8 Where next for online methods?

Predicting the future of something like online research methods is extremely difficult because it is contingent on so many other factors. However, it is possible to argue that online research methods develop in response to three main factors:

- Changes in the socio-technological world which online research seeks to investigate – in particular, the changes which emerge from the development of internet technologies and the social practices which utilize the internet.
- Changes in technical capabilities which facilitate new forms of research or offer new research tools.
- Changes in methodological thinking that emerge in relation to the above two factors and to wider developments in the epistemological traditions which inform online research methods.

In relation to changes in the socio-technological world, some commentators argue that we are currently in the midst of a period of paradigm shift, and that making meaningful predictions is essentially impossible. Fischer, Lyon and Zeitlyn therefore focus their predictions about the future of online research methods on the emergent periphery of today, using it as a basis from which to extrapolate the mainstream of the future (Fischer, Lyon and Zeitlyn 2008). Inevitably the future is built on the foundations of the present, and so this strategy is undoubtedly a good one, and one which is broadly followed in this chapter. However the 'Fischer fifteen year rule' for the mainstreaming of technology may not hold within the current environment. Shirky argues that 'the bigger the opportunity offered by new tools, the less completely anyone can extrapolate the future from the previous shape of society', and it would be worth keeping that in mind in any consideration of where the future may lead online research methods (Shirky 2010: 2552–53).

The future is therefore likely to be at once built out of the present and sufficiently different to it as to be difficult to predict accurately. Facer and Sandford argue that any attempt to predict the future is essentially a political act which seeks to shape the future it predicts (Facer and Sandford 2010). They present four principles for future enquiry which could be usefully restated in the context of the future development of online research methods:

- Explorations into the future should attempt to challenge assumptions rather than present definitive predictions.
- The future is not determined by its technologies but rather by how and why those technologies are used.
- Thinking about the future always involves values and politics.
- Research has a range of responsibilities that need to be reflected in enquires about its future. In other words, how you think the future of research will develop is bound up with what you think research is for.

Facer and Sandford then go on to use these principles to develop a series of possible socio-technical worlds, differentiated by different levels of commodification and social capital. From these possibilities, a variety of implications spring about how educators and researchers might relate to changes in the socio-technical environment.

This chapter does not attempt to map out socio-technological futures in as ambitious a way as Facer and Sandford, but there is much value in their approach. It is therefore important that the future 'predictions' advanced here are recognized for their partiality and contingency. The future will not emerge in a straight line from the present and, if it has any value, social research will be part of shaping the future as well as responding to it.

A changing context for online research methods

Predicting the future of online research methods clearly needs to be done within the context of an understanding of the wider socio-technological future. However, it is also important to attend to the local context of changes to higher education, the academic professions, research practice and methodological thinking. Unsurprisingly, higher education is being shaped by many of the factors that are shaping the wider socio-technical environment. These trends are not purely technical, and also have contestable political and conceptual elements which different researchers may relate to in different ways. Advocates of the use of social media in research argue that it has the potential to speed up the development of new ideas, make collaborations more effective and efficient, open up a channel of communication with the general public and enhance the professional networks of researchers (Cann, Dimitriou and Hooley 2011). While these ideas about the positive influence of social media on intellectual life have been challenged ideologically (Keen 2007), and questions asked about their pervasiveness (Procter, Williams and Stewart 2010), it seems unlikely that research and wider academic practices can remain unmoved whilst new technologies transform publishing, information exchange and a wide range of other social institutions and processes. How academics respond to these changes remains to be seen, but social media, the semantic web, mobile technologies and all the other socio-technical developments are likely to influence the practice of the academy in some way. If there are changes in wider academic practice, these changes are likely to manifest in the arena of social research, particularly if social media enables academic practices to become more open, collaborative and routinely engaged in the non-academic world.

The trend towards greater engagement by academics in the non-academic world can be observed in both the 'public communication' of research agenda, and in the increasing requirement for datasets used in research to be made more readily accessible to others. King argues that journals, publishers and funders should work to create a culture of data sharing as a norm (King 2011: 720). Alongside this he argues that there needs to be greater thinking put into the development of 'privacy enhanced data sharing protocols', to ensure that concepts like confidentiality do not become untenable within social science research.

The changes in the socio-technical world, and the technical capabilities that facilitate them, continue to influence methodological thinking in social research. One trend that it is possible to predict is the increased mainstreaming of online research and its re-absorbance into the methodological traditions from which it emerged. Fischer, Lyon and Zeitlyn's assertion that the 'firm distinction between online and offline research is a present phenomenon', and prediction that online research will soon cease to be 'the odd one out', seem convincing (Fischer, Lyon and Zeitlyn 2008: 520). However, whilst online research methods may move into the mainstream, it is possible to anticipate that the dialogue between research methods and cutting (or bleeding) edge technologies will continue to generate methodological challenges for researchers. The term 'online research methods' has been a useful one because it has facilitated a methodological discussion about the inter-relationship between methodology, technology and the world. At some point technical tools become familiar enough to be invisible, and the use of an online survey is seen as no more 'technological' than the use of paper, pens and clipboard. However, the tools will continue to develop and social research methods will continue to need to explore how to use, critique and understand them.

A key perspective that underpins this book is the idea that, despite differing epistemological traditions, there is methodological thinking that binds approaches to online research methods together. As this book has shown, there are very important distinctions between different online research methods. However, there is also learning that can be drawn from across different methodologies and synergies that can be achieved between them. One area that seems highly likely to generate further thinking and investigation is that of new mixed methods approaches and the further development of hybrid methods.

Symonds and Gorad argue that the use of mixed methods in the social sciences has become so widespread that there is a need to rethink the label to ensure that it is meaningful (Symonds and Gorad 2010). Examination of online research methods supports the assertion that the rigid distinctions between quantitative, qualitative and mixed methods are becoming increasingly difficult to maintain. For example, the ethnographic approaches described in chapter 6 are increasingly encountering vast and easily accessible datasets which can potentially swamp qualitative approaches. A small community of individuals can rapidly generate data across a multitude of platforms over the course of a day, and researchers seeking to track, map and analyse these data may find that quantitative tools are useful. Similarly the increase in computational power, as well as the growth of naturally occurring online datasets, may enable quantitative researchers to interrogate the kinds of issues that were previously confined to qualitative research. Fielding and Lee discuss some of these possibilities in relation to the use of Grid computing and CAQDAS (Fielding and Lee 2008).

Alongside the mixing of methods, it is also possible to observe some mixing of disciplines. Inter-disciplinarity has clearly been important in the development of online research methods, but this is not merely about the application of the same tool to different problems. Increasingly, it is difficult to decide what discipline research questions sit in – for example, is it appropriate to discuss people's use of Facebook in terms of media/ communication studies, education, computer studies, sociology or some combination of all of these? King argues that access to new sources of digital data and new analytical tools has resulted in bioscientists, computer scientists and physicists moving into realms previously inhabited by social scientists, as digital social data is analysed to answer a much wider range of questions (King 2011). The idea that there may be valuable synergies in inter-disciplinarity and mixed or hybrid methods is not a new one, nor is it confined to online research methods. However, there are a number of features of the online environment that may serve to focus the minds of researchers on synergies between different approaches. This is not to say that technology will wash away epistemological positions that have political and ideological components as well as technical ones, but it may be the case that the shifting environment frames methodological discussions in new ways that open up the possibility of new formations emerging.

The rest of this chapter examines how changes in the technical capability of particular tools or sets of tools are reframing methodological thinking. In particular it examines the idea of visualization of naturally occurring data, the combination of datasets, the growth of the diverse and integrated web, and the development of new forms of technically supported participation in research. These trends all seem important, but the list is not meant to be an exhaustive one. The opportunities that exist for new tools to reframe methodological thinking are likely to continue to expand in ways that we cannot predict or fully comprehend.

Visualizing naturally occurring data

The process of utilizing naturally occurring data is not new, as chapter 6 has already shown in relation to ethnographic and qualitative methods. For researchers, this presents some enormous opportunities as long as the technical and ethical challenges can successfully be negotiated. King argues that this massive increase in available social data enables researchers to address 'major, previously intractable problems that affect human society' (King 2011: 719). Developing methodological approaches which make use of this enormous resource is likely to be a key area of development over the next few years.

There is a tradition of quantitative research in this area which has typically used tools like Issue Crawler to undertake network analysis around the inter-relationships between different websites (Xenos and Bennett 2007). However, with the growing use of social networks, increasing amounts of human experience are available in the form of naturally occurring data. So, for example, Mislove *et al.* have investigated the social structures that are evident through a quantitative examination of social media data, and used these to predict the attributes of members of that network (Mislove, Viswanath, Gummadi and Druschel 2010).

As the tools become more powerful, it is possible to begin to use quantitative visualization tools to interrogate large datasets and see how they work (Blondel, Guillaume, Lambiotte and Lefebvre 2008). Visualizations draw on the ability to identify pattern and structure, and represent these visually as a distribution of data points. This can provide a starting point from which to focus more powerful statistical tools and deeper qualitative enquiry on areas of interest (Merico, Gfeller and Bader 2009). Interactive visualization tools, used as part of an analytic process, allow real-time visual dialogue with data (Zudilova-Seinstra, Adriaansen and Liere 2009).

The ability to visualize social networks as a part of data analysis opens up the possibility for much more subtle approaches. For example, the opportunity to identify issues, focus in on them and reframe the analysis in the light of developments in real time enables social researchers to deal with the ever increasing volume and complexity of online data. The real-time visualization and analysis of large-scale datasets also provides a new basis on which mutually informing mixed methods approaches can be built, as part of an analytical move between large-scale and close analysis of detail.

Combining data

A second promising area is the ability to combine and relate a range of different online data. So, for example, market researchers examining consumer behaviour through an analysis of customer databases might seek to broaden their understanding of the behaviour of consumers by relating customer records to interests recorded by the same individuals in their Facebook profile, or the occupational information that they list on LinkedIn. In this example, consumers are suddenly transformed from a series of records of purchases into complex individuals with lives, interests, relationships and histories. If the complexity of this new combined dataset can be managed, its explanatory power is likely to be huge.

Linking together different datasets is often described as a mash-up, and it has huge potential for researchers. The ability to relate datasets to wider contextual information is a key activity undertaken in the analysis of social research data. Mash-ups provide an opportunity to bring context into data analysis in a far more systematic way than has previously been possible. However, again there are clearly ethical issues in building these kinds of multi-dimensional datasets. O'Hara and Shadbolt describe how public data in the US relating to sex offenders has been mashed with geographical data to allow the creation of an interactive map which can allow you to pinpoint your nearest sex offenders and to see pictures of them (O'Hara and Shadbolt 2008: 152). Two datasets (offender information and map data) are combined together with search criteria (for example, the search term 'sex offender') to create a new dataset that is much more powerful than any of the constituent parts. For public policy this throws up huge challenges, as surveillance of individuals becomes routine and previously private information becomes available to the state, private companies, the media and crucially to other interested individuals (Kerr, Lucock and Steeves 2009).

For researchers, there is considerable power in the ability to combine existing data together in meaningful ways, but this correspondingly throws up further concerns for researchers around issues such as confidentiality and anonymity. However, despite the ethical difficulties the potential remains, and is further enabled by the increasingly common practice of linking together various online accounts to ensure a single login point.

The ability to link datasets is helped by the development of semantic standards such as the Resource Description Framework (RDF) (W3C 1999). By agreeing on common metadata approaches, the ability to build meaningful links between different datasets is enhanced, and new forms of analysis enabled. Perhaps one of the most powerful ways in which the opportunity to combine distinct datasets might aid researchers is through the use of geographical information. Fischer, Lyon and Zeitlyn discuss the possibility of researchers making use of the GPS data that many devices record, but this only scratches the surface of possible uses of geographical data that are derived from online data sets (Fischer, Lyon and Zeitlyn 2008). As O'Hara and Shadbolt's sex offenders example demonstrates, the rendering and exploration of the spatial elements of datasets has become increasingly possible (O'Hara and Shadbolt 2008).

The decision by mainstream geographical information providers (such as the UK's Ordnance Survey) to adopt standards such as RDF (Goodwin, Dolbear and Hart 2008) massively increases the quality and inter-operability of such data, opening up new possibilities for researchers. These include the ability to examine the interplay between geographical and online space. Nag argues that research into online phenomena may be missing important factors if it does not acknowledge the geographical distribution and locations in which online things take place (Nag 2010). Until recently it was highly difficult to identify geographical space in a meaningful way; however, through the use of GPS technologies and standards such as RDF, researchers now have the tools to explore this further.

The diverse and integrated internet

The discussion of geographical data draws attention to the fact that the internet is now accessed from a wide range of different devices which enable new blends of online and onsite research. The introduction discussed the fact that 'cyberia' is no longer a place that people visit, remote from their everyday lives – rather, the internet intersects with people's onsite lives in an increasing range of ways. Mobile phones, electronic reading devices and tablet computers are becoming ever more common, but these are only the tip of the iceberg of internet connectivity that is reshaping the social world and which therefore may ultimately be re-purposed by online researchers.

It is possible to describe the internet as being at once diverse and integrated. Users connect into the same architecture and access much of the same content (integrated), but utilize an increasing range of devices to do this (diverse). This led Anderson and Wolff to declare, 'The Web is Dead. Long live the internet', and to argue that the web will no longer provide the main way in which people interact online (Anderson and Wolff 2010). For online researchers this may initially make things more complex, as the careful development of web-based translations of research methods will need to be reworked for the new platforms and devices through which people are experiencing the online environment. Furthermore, if Anderson and Wolff's predictions are right, there may also be a trend towards enclosing the essentially open and free nature of online space which may in turn have impacts, particularly for cash-poor public sector social researchers.

Researchers have already been making use of a wide range of diverse and integrated devices. Hagen *et al.* set out a typology of research methods for understanding mobile technology use (Hagen, Robertson, Kan and Sadler 2005). They note that researchers can understand participants' behaviour in a variety of ways such as using data logs recorded by mobile devices or by asking them to wear cameras or sensors. Increasingly, these research approaches are being applied to broader research questions that are less directly connected to the ergonomics of mobile phone use. So Vavoula and Sharples used mobile devices to assess young people's interaction with museum exhibitions (Vavoula and Sharples 2009), Aanensen *et al.* used smartphones to collect geographically tagged field data (Aanensen, Huntley, Feil, Own and Spratt, 2009), and Eagle, Pentland and Lazer used mobile phone data to investigate people's social networks by looking at factors such as physical proximity (Eagle, Pentland and Lazer 2009).

While the most obvious manifestation of the diverse and integrated internet is the explosion of increasingly computer-like mobile devices, the implications are actually much broader. The technical literature discusses technologies such as wearable computing (Van Laerhoven 2011); radio frequency identification (RFID) tags which enable the onsite world to be perceived as part of the online world (O'Hara and Shadbolt 2008: 203–09); online monitoring of embedded systems (Wood, Stankovic, Virone, Selavo, He, Cao, Doan, Wu, Fang and Stoleru 2008). Many of the technical details are not important in the context of this work, but the political and social implications are critical. The diverse and integrated internet is the vehicle through which ever greater integration between the online and onsite worlds is being delivered. For researchers, this clearly raises research questions, methodological possibilities, and considerable ethical and conceptual challenges.

Allowing participants to really participate

Much discussion around current technological trends emphasises the egalitarian and democratizing nature of social media and other Web 2.0 technologies (Tapscott and Williams 2006; Howe 2008; Shirky 2009; Shirky 2010). While this enthusiasm for the political and economic outcomes of social media has been critiqued (Carr 2010; Lanier 2010), and there is clearly need for empirical investigation of some of the techno-utopianism, the perspective remains both influential and appealing.

Much of the current theorization of the social web draws on O'Reilly's paper which examined the conceptual basis of the Web 2.0 approach to technical development (O'Reilly 2005). O'Reilly's paper emphasised the contingency of all technologies, and encouraged an open, nimble approach that viewed development as a process rather than a destination. Crucially O'Reilly also emphasised collaboration and the idea of co-production with users. Rathi and Givens used O'Reilly's article as a lens through which social research could be viewed as an analogous activity to web development (Rathi and Givens 2010). They therefore emphasise enhanced collaboration (perhaps sharing coding tasks across the web), and a more participatory form of engagement with research participants.

The decision to involve participants in research raises deeper epistemological questions. Is the role of a researcher to produce knowledge out of the raw materials gathered from participants, or is all social research essentially a form of co-production? The answers that researchers give to this again depend on political and epistemological positioning. However, in the past, researchers who sought ongoing, meaningful dialogue with participants had to overcome considerable logistical and financial obstacles. Even disseminating results to participants in an appropriate form could be costly and challenging, while deeper engagement with participants, especially during the analysis stage was more difficult still (Doherty and Price 1998; Pain and Francis 2003).

For those conducting research online the issue of participation and co-production presents very different challenges. Whereas the onsite researcher was frequently geographically removed from his or her participants, the online researcher remains easily accessible even after the conclusion of the project. This accessibility can be enhanced through connections built with participants through social networks etc., and clearly has the potential to blur boundaries in the nature of the researcher/ participant relationship. Even if a researcher does not actively build a relationship with the research participants, if they discuss or publish research outputs that might be of interest to participants these may appear in online searches, and participants/subjects may discover and engage with research that speaks to their experience in some way.

The idea of democratization of research, in which an empowered participant engages in the co-production of research findings, is a political and methodological ideal which is becoming increasingly possible. Cooke and Buckley argue that a 'combination of social computing tools with an understanding of social networks' will allow market researchers to 'build new types of research community in which respondents interact not only with researchers but with the clients and, most fertilely, with each other' (Cooke and Buckley 2008: 271). In the kind of situation that Cooke and Buckley describe, professional researchers and research funders are likely to need to cede some control to the participants that they are working with. While not all researchers will advocate this kind of approach to research, it may be that they experience participants becoming more assertive and demanding greater access to research outputs than is currently the case.

In summary

The future of online research methods is inevitably difficult to predict. However, given the trajectory of the field it seems likely that it will be a bright one, and that the idea of undertaking social research online will continue to become more mainstream. However, it is important to recognize that online research methods have developed in close conversation with wider socio-technological changes. It is expected that these wider changes will exert even greater influence on the development of social research methods than the online research methods tradition itself.

In particular, the explosion in online and digital data sources has the potential to reframe the nature of social research by placing vast amounts of naturally occurring data in the hands of researchers. Whether the methodologies outlined in this book (surveys, interviews and focus groups, ethnographies and experiments) continue to be the best way to describe the online social research that emerges in the future remains to be seen. This chapter has suggested that social researchers will discover increasing possibilities in the visualization of online data, the opportunity to combine different data sources, the diverse and integrated nature of the internet, and increased opportunities for participatory research enabled by social tools. This list is far from exhaustive but, as with any attempt at prediction, the most exciting possibilities are likely to lie beyond what can currently be seen.

Further reading

There are a large number of people writing about the future of technology or the internet. *A History of the Internet and the Digital Future* (Ryan 2010), *The Future of the Internet: And How to Stop It* (Zittrain 2009) and *Cognitive Surplus* (Shirky 2010) all provide good, if strongly opinionated starting points for thinking about what the socio-technological implications of new technologies might be.

Glossary

One of the principal challenges in undertaking online research is the need to penetrate the language. The challenges associated with unpicking a new methodological approach are compounded by the inter-disciplinary nature of the field. Discussions around methodological approaches often require researchers to recognize that they are drawing on different theoretical paradigms and disciplinary traditions.

In addition to unpicking the language of inter-disciplinary methodological debate, this glossary also demystifies the technological terminology that the online researcher is required to master. Understanding the wide range of tools, environments and online cultures within which online research is conducted is an essential precursor to undertaking online research.

Anonymity refers to a situation when no one, including the researcher, can relate a participant's identity to any information related to the project.

ARG (Alternative Reality Game). This is an interactive narrative, often involving various media and game elements to tell a story which could be influenced by participants' actions or suggestions.

Asynchronous is used to describe communications which are not required to take place at a set time. The data can be transmitted intermittently rather than in a steady stream. For example, an asynchronous online interview will usually involve the interviewer posting to a discussion list or emailing interview questions to respondents to answer at their own convenience. Neither party needs to be online at the same time.

Avatar is the graphical depiction of an individual online. It is commonly applied to characters used in virtual reality or online gaming environments.

Bandwidth is a measure of the amount of data that can be sent through a connection, usually described in kilobits per second (Kbs).

Bleeding edge is a way of describing new and innovative technologies. The metaphor of 'bleeding' is often used instead of the more conventional 'cutting' to suggest a process that involves more risk and less precision.

Blogs are websites composed of serial short or medium length entries. Most blogs are interactive, allowing visitors to leave comments and even message each other via widgets on the blogs, and it is this interactivity that distinguishes them from other static websites. Blogs may be maintained by individuals or a collaborating group.

Bulletin board is another term for a discussion board.

CAQDAS (Computer Assisted Qualitative Data Analysis Software). A range of software applications that aid in the analysis of qualitative data.

Chat room Chat is a facility allowing real-time text-based communication between two or more users in virtual places known as 'chat rooms'. This usually makes use of IRC (Internet Relay Chat) technology.

Confidentiality describes the situation where the researchers know the participant's identity, but has undertaken not to reveal it to others.

Discussion board is a web application that allows asynchronous communication to take place. Users post messages which are displayed to all those with access to the board. People can then reply or add to the messages, continuing the discussion in a 'thread' of related postings. Also known as bulletin boards, discussion groups or web/internet forums.

Email Electronic mail, commonly called email or e-mail, is a method of sending and receiving digital information or messages from one user to another.

Flaming General term for aggressive or insulting messages or posts. A **Flame War** is used to describe a situation in which an online discussion becomes a series of aggressive exchanges or personal attacks.

Focus groups are a specialized form of group interview in which participants are asked to interact around a particular theme or set of issues. Participants are often selected to be representative of a particular population. Typically focus groups seek to reveal opinions, attitudes, beliefs and reactions rather than to establish facts.

Forums/bulletin boards Different terms for discussion board.

GPS (Global Positioning System) is a 'constellation' of twenty-four well-spaced satellites that orbit Earth and make it possible for people with ground receivers to pinpoint their geographic location. The location accuracy is anywhere from 100 to 10 meters for most equipment. GPS equipment is widely used in science, and has now become sufficiently low-cost so that almost anyone can own a GPS receiver.

Grid A distributed computer infrastructure that combines parallel and distributed computer platforms to enable computational operations exceeding the capabilities of individual desktop computers.

Group interviews use a similar approach to individual interviews, but apply it to a group. It would be common for the group to comprise individuals with a shared characteristic or background. Data is derived from the groups' answers to the questions, but also from their interactions with each other.

Internet A global public system of interconnected computer networks.

Interviews involve an interaction between a researcher and a research participant for the purpose of gathering qualitative data. Interviews typically gather both factual and interpretative data, and can use a variety of different approaches (structured/unstructured, life history, thematic etc).

IP address (also known as 'IP number' or simply 'IP'). This is a code made up of numbers separated by three dots that identifies a particular computer on the internet. Every computer, whether it be a web server or your home computer, requires an IP address to connect to the internet. IP addresses consist of four sets of numbers from 0 to 255, separated by three dots.

IRC (Internet Relay Chat). This is a form of real-time (synchronous) digital communication. IRC is often used by groups on discussion forums, but this type of 'chat' can also be used on a one-to-one basis to send private messages.

Lists, listserves or email lists A list or listserve is a specialized use of email in which individuals or groups distribute information to a wide-spread group of internet users by using list of email addresses. This works in the same way that a traditional mailing list might be employed to send information to a group of subscribers. The Listserve itself is owned by a specific software company and is a registered trademark.

Lurking The act of watching others contributing to an online forum, discussion or network without contributing.

Mash-ups are web pages or applications that integrate complementary elements from two or more sources.

Micro-blogs A medium which allows users to broadcast short entries (typically 140 characters or less) in the form of a text, a picture or a very short video clip to other users of the service.

MMOG (Massively Multi-player Online Game). This is an online video game that is capable of supporting hundreds or thousands of players simultaneously.

MMORPGS (Massively Multi-Player Online Role-playing game). *See* MMOG.

MOO A particular form of MUD based around programming conventions descended from the original MOO server.

MUDs (Multi-user Dimensions). An online gaming environment similar to a MMOG but usually based around text interactions.

Offline The state of not being connected to the internet.

Online The state of being connected to the internet.

Onsite A description of activities which do not require the internet.

Playspaces Sometimes referred to as massively multi-player online games (MMOGS). Other acronyms include MMORPGS, ARG, MUD & MOO.

Populations are the total group of people being studied. Researchers will commonly be unable to interact with everyone being studied (the population), and will therefore need to work with a sample.

Questionnaires are tools or instruments which researchers use to undertake a survey. They usually comprise a series of questions or stimulus for response.

RDF (Resource Description Framework). This has come to be used as a general method for conceptual description or modelling of information that is implemented in web resources, using a variety of syntax formats.

Recruitment is used to describe the ways in which participants are encouraged to take part in the researcher's survey.

Response rates describe the number of people who participated in a survey in relation to the number of people in the sample. It is often expressed as a percentage.

RFID (Radio frequency identification). This generic term is used to describe a system that transmits the identity (in the form of a unique serial number) of an object or person wirelessly, using radio waves. It's grouped under the broad category of automatic identification technologies.

Samples are part of a population which is examined for the purpose of drawing inferences about the population as a whole. Quantitative researchers may use statistical techniques to determine their sample and to analyse the data they gather.

Second Life An online virtual world developed by Linden Lab.

Social bookmarking Services which allow users to store, tag, organize, share and search for bookmarks (links) to resources online. Unlike file sharing, the resources themselves are not shared, only bookmarks which point to them.

Social media Term used to describe a variety of web-based platforms, applications and technologies that enable people to socially interact with one another online. Some examples of social media sites and applications include Facebook, YouTube, Del.icio.us, Twitter, Digg, blogs and other sites that have content based on user participation and user-generated content (UGC).

Social news websites allow users to submit links and vote them up or down. These sites are generally designed so the content that gets voted up the most is rewarded with more exposure on the site.

Social software (also called social networking software) enables social computing, i.e. it enables people to rendezvous, connect or collaborate through computer-mediated communication and to form online communities.

Social tools (sometimes called social software) are software and platforms that enable participatory culture – for example, blogs, podcasts, forums, wikis and shared videos and presentations.

Surveys are research methods used by researchers to collect data. They can be either quantitative or qualitative in focus or a mixture of the two.

Synchronous is used to describe communications which take place in 'real time' in an environment such as an internet chat room. A good example of this is online interviews, where all participants must be online simultaneously and questions and answers are posted in a way which mimics a traditional interview.

Usernet is a public access network on the internet that provides group discussions and group e-mail. It is a giant, dispersed bulletin board that is maintained by volunteers who provide news and mail feeds to other nodes. All content that travels over the internet is called 'NetNews'. A running collection of messages about a particular subject is called a 'newsgroup'.

Video-conferencing is when telecommunication technologies are used for two or more locations to communicate and interact at the same time via two-way video and audio transmissions.

Virtual worlds are online communities where users can interrelate with each other and use and create various objects. Typically, virtual worlds take the form of a computer based simulated environment.

VLE (Virtual Learning Environment). A system which is designed to work over the internet to provide support for teaching and learning in educational settings.

VR (Virtual Reality) can be defined as a synthetic or virtual environment which gives a person a sense of reality. This definition would include any synthetic environment which gives a person a feeling of 'being there'. VR generally refers to environments which are computer generated, although there are several immersive environments which are not entirely synthesized by computer.

Web 2.0 A popular buzzword among the technical and marketing communities, used to describe a perceived ongoing trend in the use of world wide web technology and web design, which emphasizes the importance of information-sharing, creativity and collaboration among internet users. It is regarded by some as the next phase in the internet's evolution, although the term (coined in 2004 by O'Reilly Media) refers to changes in the ways existing internet facilities are used, rather than to an actual 'second generation' of web technology. The increased use of interactive internet-based services such as social networking sites, blogs, video-sharing sites, wikis and forums has led to a movement away from static, read-only webpages towards dynamic websites whose content is shaped partially or entirely by their users, and for this reason, Web 2.0 is sometimes called 'internet with a human face'.

Web/www (world wide web) Part of the internet that contains linked text, image, sound and video documents. Before www, information-retrieval on the internet was text-based and required that users know basic UNIX commands. The web has gained popularity largely because of its ease of use (point-and-click graphical interface) and multi-media capabilities, as well as its convenient access to other types of internet services (such as e-mail, Telnet and Usenet).

Web conference pages Designed to facilitate synchronous communication and collaboration for geographically distributed participants. Operates on standard desktop computers communicating on the public internet; no special-purpose hardware (beyond web cam or microphone) is required. Typically, the software runs in a web browser.

Wikis are collaborative websites that can be directly edited by anyone with appropriate permission.

WoW (World of Warcraft). A massively multi-player online role-playing game (MMORPG) by Blizzard Entertainment, a subsidiary of Activision Blizzard. It is the fourth released game set in the fantasy Warcraft universe, which was first introduced by *Warcraft: Orcs & Humans* in 1994.

WYSIWYG A display generated by word-processing or desktop-publishing software that exactly reflects the appearance of the printed document.

Bibliography

All material referenced in the bibliography is available through the online social bookmarking tool Citeulike: http://www.citeulike.org/user/iCeGS/ tag/online%5fresearch%5fmethods
This citeulike tag will continue to be updated after the publication of the book, to provide a living bibliography for the project.

Aanensen, D.M., Huntley, D.M., Feil, E.J., Own, F. and Spratt, B.G. (2009), 'EpiCollect: Linking smartphones to web applications for epidemiology, ecology and community data collection', *PLoS ONE*, 4(9): e6968. http://dx.doi.org/10.1371/journal.pone.0006968 [accessed 28 Feb 2012].

Alastalo, M. (2008), 'The history of social research methods', in P. Alasuutari, L. Bickman, and J. Brannen (eds.), *The Sage Handbook of Social Research Methods*, London: Sage Publications, 26–41.

Alasuutari, P. (2004), 'The globalization of qualitative research', in C. Seale, G. Gobo, J.F. Gubrium and D. Silverman (eds.), *Qualitative Research Practice*, London: Sage Publications, 595–608.

Allen, C. (1996), 'What's wrong with the "Golden Rule?" Conundrums of conducting ethical research in Cyberspace', *The Information Society*, 12(2): 175–88.

Anderson, C. and Wolff, M. (2010), 'The web is dead. Long live the internet', *Wired*, 17 August 2010.

Anderson, L. (2006), 'Analytic autoethnography', *Journal of Contemporary Ethnography*, 35(4): 373–95.

Anderson, S.E. and Gansneder, B.M. (1995), 'Using electronic mail surveys and computer monitored data for studying computer mediated communication systems', *Social Science Computer Review*, 13(1): 33–46.

Arnau, R.C., Thompson, R.L. and Cook, C. (2001), 'Do different response formats change the latent structure of responses? An empirical investigation using taxometric analysis', *Educational and Psychological Measurement*, 61(1): 23–44.

Avery, A.J., Savelyich, B.S., Sheikh, A., Cantrill, Morris, C.J., Fernando, B., Bainbridge, M., Horsfield, P. and Teasdale, S. (2005), 'Identifying and establishing consensus on the most important safety features of GP computer systems: e-Delphi study', *Informatics in Primary Care*, 13(1): 3–12.

Babbie, E.R. (1990), *Survey Research Methods* (2nd ed.), Belmont, CA: Wadsworth Publishing.

Banks, M. (2001), *Visual Methods in Social Research*, London: Sage Publications.

Barchard, K.A. and Williams, J. (2008), 'Practical advice for conducting ethical online experiments and questionnaires for United States psychologists', *Behavior Research Methods*, 40(4): 1111–28.

Barratt, M.J. and Lenton, S. (2010), 'Beyond recruitment? Participatory online research with people who use drugs', *International Journal of Internet Ethics*, 3(1): 69–86.

Batinic, B., Reips, U.-D. and Bosnjak, M. (ed.) (2002), *Online Social Sciences*, Cambridge: Hogrefe and Huber.

Baym, N.K. (1995), 'From Practice to Culture on Usenet', in S.L. Star (ed.) *The Cultures of Computing, 29–52, Sociological Review Monograph Series*, London: Basil Blackwell.

Beaudouin V. and Velkovska J. (1999), 'The Cyberians: an Empirical Study of Sociality in a Virtual Community', in K. Buckner (ed.), *Proceedings of Esprit i3 Workshop on Ethnographic Studies in Real and Virtual Environments: Inhabited Information Spaces and Connected Communities*, Edinburgh: Inhabited Information Spaces and Connected Communities, 102–12.

Beaulieu, A. (2004), 'Mediating ethnography: objectivity and the making of ethnographies of the internet', *Social Epistemology*, 18(2–3): 139–63.

Berg, B. L. (2008), *Qualitative Research Methods for the Social Sciences* (7th ed.), London: Pearson.

Bertrand, C. and Bourdeau, L. (2010), 'Research Interviews by Skype: A new Data Collection Method', *Proceedings of the 9th European Conference on Research Methodology for Business and Management Studies*, IE Business School, Madrid, Spain 24–25 June 2010. http://www.academic-conferences.org/pdfs/ECRM10-abstract%20booklet.pdf [accessed 28 Feb 2012].

Best, S.J. and Krueger, B.S. (2004), 'Internet Data Collection', *Sage Publications University Paper 141*, London: Sage Publications.

Birnbaum, M.H. (2000), 'Designing online experiments', in M.H. Birnbaum (ed.), *Psychological Experiments on the Internet*, San Diego: Academic Press.

Blondel, V.D., Guillaume, J.-L., Lambiotte, R. and Lefebvre, E. (2008), 'Fast unfolding of communities in large networks', *Journal of Statistical Mechanics: Theory and Experiment*, 10, P10008, 1–12.

Boehlefeld, S.P. (1996), 'Doing the Right Thing: Ethical Cyberspace Research', *The Information Society*, 12(2): 141–52.

Boellstorff, T. (2006), 'A ludicrous discipline? Ethnography and game studies', *Games and Culture*, 1(1): 29–35.

Bos, N., Karahalios, K., Chávez, M.M., Poole, E.S., Thomas, J.C. and Yardi, S. (2009), 'Research ethics in the Facebook era: privacy, anonymity, and oversight', *Proceedings of the 27th international conference extended abstracts on Human factors in computing systems*, CHI EA '09, New York: ACM, 2767–70.

Bowker, N. and Tuffin, K. (2003), 'Dicing with deception: People with disabilities' strategies for managing safety and identity online', *Journal of Computer-Mediated Communication*, 8(2).

Boyd, D. and Ellison, N.B. (2007), 'Social network sites: Definition, history, and scholarship', *Journal of Computer-Mediated Communication*, 13(1): 210–30.

Boyd, D. and Heer, J. (2006), 'Profiles as Conversation: Networked Identity Performance on Friendster', in *Proceedings of the Hawai'i International Conference on System Sciences (HICSS-39), Persistent Conversation Track*, Kauai, HI: IEEE Computer Society, 4–7 January, 2006.

Brewer, J. (2001), *Ethnography*, Buckingham: Open University Press.

Brotherson, M.J. (1994), 'Interactive focus group interviewing: A qualitative research method in early intervention', *Topics in Early Childhood Special Education*, 14(1): 101–18.

Bruckman, A. (2004), 'Opportunities and Challenges in Methodology and Ethics', in M.D. Johns, S.-L.S. Chen, G.J. Hall (eds.), *Online Social Research: Methods, Issues and Ethics*, New York: Peter Lang.

Brüggen, E. and Willems, P. (2009), 'A critical comparison of offline focus groups, online focus groups and e–Delphi', *International Journal of Market Research*, 51(3): 363–81.

Buchanan, T. (2007), 'Personality testing on the internet', in A.N. Joinson, K.Y.A. McKenna, T. Postmes and U.-D. Reips (ed.), *Oxford Handbook of Internet Psychology (Oxford Library of Psychology)*, Oxford: Oxford University Press, 447–59.

Buckingham, A. and Saunders, P. (2004), *The Survey Methods Workbook: From Design to Analysis*, Cambridge: Polity Press.

Bull, S.S., Breslin, L.T., Wright, E.E., Black, S.R., Levine, D. and Santelli, J.S. (2011), 'Case study: An ethics case study of HIV prevention research on Facebook: The Just/Us study', *Journal of Pediatric Psychology*, 36(10): 1082–92.

Bullard, J. and O'Brien, H.L. (2011), 'Online synchronous interviewing of the info-savvy', in *Proceedings of the 2011 iConference*, iConference '11, New York: ACM, 649–50.

Burger, N., Charness, G. and Lynham, J. (2011), 'Field and online experiments on self-control', *Journal of Economic Behavior and Organization*, 77(3): 393–404.

Burke, M., Kraut, R. and Marlow, C. (2011), 'Social capital on Facebook: differentiating uses and users', in *Proceedings of the 2011 annual conference on Human factors in computing systems* , CHI '11, New York: ACM, 571–80.

Busher, H. (2001), 'Being and Becoming a Doctoral Student: Culture, Literacies and Self–identity', paper presented at TESOL Arabia Conference, 14–16 March.

Cann, A., Dimitriou, K. and Hooley, T. (2011), *Social Media: A Guide for Researchers*, London: Research Information Network.

Cantrell, M.A. and Lupinacci, P. (2007), 'Methodological issues in online data collection', *Journal of Advanced Nursing*, 60(5): 544–49.

Cantrell, M.A. and Lupinacci, P. (2008), 'Investigating the determinants of health-related quality of life among childhood cancer survivors', *Journal of Advanced Nursing*, 6(1): 73–83.

Carr, N. (2010), *The Shallows*, Atlantic Books.

Carrick-Davies, S. (2011), *Munch Poke Ping! Vulnerable Young People, Social-Media and E-Safety*. Training and Development Agency. http://www.carrick-davies.com/downloads/Munch_Poke_Ping_-_E-Safety_and_Vulnerable_Young_People_FULL_REPORT.pdf [accessed 28 Feb 2012].

Carter, D. (2005), 'Living in virtual communities: An ethnography of human relationships in cyberspace', *Information, Communication and Society*, 8(2): 148–67.

Carusi, A. (2008), 'Data as representation: beyond anonymity in E-research ethics', *International Journal of Internet Research Ethics*, 1(1): 37–65.

Charlesworth, A. (2008), 'Understanding and managing legal issues in internet research', in N. Fielding, R.M. Lee and G. Black (eds.), *The Handbook of Online Research Methods*, Thousand Oaks, CA: Sage Publications, 42–47.

Chen, S.-L.S., Hall, G.J. and Johns, M.D. (2004), 'Research paparazzi in cyberspace: The voices of the researched', in M.D. Johns, S.-L.S. Chen and G.J. Hall (eds.) (2004) *Online Social Research: Methods, Issues, and Ethics*. New York: Peter Lang, 157–75.

Chenail, R.J. (2011), 'Qualitative researchers in the blogosphere: Using blogs as diaries and data', *The Qualitative Report*, 16(1). http://www.nova.edu/ssss/QR/QR16–1/blog.pdf [accessed 28 Feb 2012].

Chu, H. (1994), E-mail in scientific communication, in M.E. Williams (ed.), *Proceedings of 1994 National Online Meeting*, New York: Learned Information, 77–86.

CNN (2009), 'Facebook faces furor over content rights'. http://www.cnn.com/2009/TECH/02/17/facebook.terms.service/index.html [accessed 28 Feb 2012].

Comley, P. (1996), 'The use of the internet as a data collection method', ESOMAR/EMAC Symposium, Edinburgh, November 1996.

Computer Industry Almanac (2010), 'Mobile PCs In-Use Surpass 200M. Over 25% of Worldwide PCs Are Mobile PCs', Arlington Heights, Illinois: Computer Industry Almanac. http://www.c-i-a.com/pr0605.htm [accessed 28 Feb 2012].

Converse, P.D., Wolfe, E.W., Huang, X. and Oswald, F.L. (2008), 'Response rates for Mixed-Mode surveys using mail and E-mail/Web, *American Journal of Evaluation*, 29(1): 99–107.

Cooke, M. and Buckley, N. (2008), 'Web 2.0, social networks and the future of market research', *International Journal of Market Research*, 50(2), 267–92.

Coomber, R. (1997), 'Using the internet for survey research', *Sociological Research Online*, 2(2): 1–14.

Correll, S. (1995), 'The ethnography of an electronic bar: the lesbian café', *Journal of Contemporary Ethnography*, 24(3): 270–98.

Cosley, D., Frankowski, D., Terveen, L., and Riedl, J. (2007), 'SuggestBot: Using Intelligent Task Routing to Help People Find Work in Wikipedia', in *Proceedings of IUI 2007*.

Couper, M.P. (2007), 'Issues of Representation in eHealth Research (with a Focus on Web Surveys)', *American Journal of Preventive Medicine*, 32(5): S83–S89.

Couper, M.P. (2008), *Designing Effective Web Surveys*, Cambridge: Cambridge University.

Couper, M.P. (2000), Web surveys: A review of issues and approaches, *Public Opinion Quarterly*, 64(4): 464–94.

Crawford, S.D., Couper, M.P. and Lamias, M.J. (2001), 'Web-surveys: Perceptions of burdens', *Social Science Computer Review*, 19(2): 146–62.

Crawford, S., McCabe, S.E. and Pope, D. (2005), 'Applying Web-Based Survey Design Standards', *Journal of Prevention and Intervention in the Community*, 29(1): 43–66.

Creswell, J.W. (2003), *Research Design: Qualitative, Quantitative, and Mixed Methods Approaches* (2nd ed.), Thousand Oaks, CA: Sage Publications.

Creswell, J.W. (2005), *Educational Research: Planning, Conducting, and Evaluating Quantitative and Qualitative research*, Upper Saddle River, NJ: Pearson.

Czaja, R.F. and Blair, J.E. (eds.), (2004), *Designing Surveys: A Guide to Decisions and Procedures (Undergraduate Research Methods and Statistics in the Social Sciences, 464)* (2nd ed.), Thousand Oaks, CA: Pine Forge Press.

Dandurand, F., Shultz, T. and Onishi, K. (2008), Comparing online and lab methods in a problem-solving experiment, *Behavior Research Methods*, 40(2): 428–34.

Danet, B., Bechar-Israeli, T., Cividalli, A. and Rosenbaum, T.Y. (1995), 'Curtain time 20:00 GMT: Experiments with virtual theater on internet relay chat', *Journal of Computer-Mediated Communication*, 1(2).

Darley J.M. and Batson C.D. (1973), 'From Jerusalem to Jericho: A study of situational and dispositional variables in helping behaviour', *Journal of Personality and Social Psychology*, 27(1):100–08.

Davis, M., Bolding, G., Hart, G., Sherr, L. and Elford, J. (2004), 'Reflecting on the experience of interviewing online: perspectives from the internet and HIV study in London,' *AIDS Care: Psychological and Socio-medical Aspects of AIDS/HIV*, 16 (8): 944–52.

Dean, B. (2009), *Urarina Society, Cosmology, and History in Peruvian Amazonia*, Florida: University Press of Florida.

Deggs, D., Grover, K. and Kacirek, K. (2010), 'Using message Publications boards to conduct online focus groups', *The Qualitative Report*, 15(4): 1026–37. http://www.nova.edu/ssss/QR/QR15–4/deggs.pdf [accessed 28 Feb 2012].

de Landsheere, G. (1997), 'History of Educational Research', in J. Keeves (ed.), *Educational Research, Methodology, and Measurement: An International Handbook* (2nd ed), Cambridge: Pergamon.

Deutskens, E., de Ruyter, K., Wetzels, M. and Oosterveld, P. (2004), 'Response rate and response quality of internet-based surveys: An experimental study', *Marketing Letters*, 15(1): 21–36.

Digital Methods Initiative (2011), https://wiki.digitalmethods.net/Dmi/WebHome [accessed 28 Feb 2012].

Digital Research Tools wiki (DiRT) (2011), https://digitalresearchtools.pbworks.com/w/page/17801672/FrontPage [accessed 28 Feb 2012].

Dillman, D.A. (2000), *Mail and Internet Surveys. The Tailored Design Method*, New York: John Wiley.

Dillman, D.A., Phelps, G., Tortora, R., Swift, K., Kohrell, J., Berck, J. and Messer, B.L. (2009), 'Response rate and measurement differences in mixed-mode surveys using mail, telephone, interactive voice response (IVR) and the internet', *Social Science Research*, 38(1): 1–18.

Dillman, D.A., Smyth, J.D. and Christian, L.M. (2008), *Internet, Mail, and Mixed-Mode Surveys: The Tailored Design Method* (3rd ed.), London: Wiley.

Dillman, D.A., Tortora, R.D. and Bowker, D. (1998), 'Principles for Constructing Web Surveys', *SESRC Technical Report 98–50*, Washington: Pullman.

Dodd, J. (1998), 'Market research on the internet – threat or opportunity?' *Marketing and Research Today*, 26(1): 60–66.

Doherty, J. and Price, M. (1998), 'The cost implications of participatory research. Experience of a health services review in a rural region in South Africa, *South African medical journal (Suid-Afrikaanse tydskrif vir geneeskunde)*, 88(3 Suppl): 390–93.

Dolnicar, S., Laesser, C. and Matus, K. (2009), 'Online versus paper', *Journal of Travel Research*, 47(3): 295–316.

Doostdar, A. (2004), '"The vulgar spirit of blogging": On language, culture, and power in Persian weblogestan', *American Anthropologist*, 106(4): 651–62.

Dougherty, H. (March 15, 2010), 'Facebook Reaches Top Ranking in US', Experian Hitwise (blog). http://weblogs.hitwise.com/heather-dougherty/2010/03/facebook_reaches_top_ranking_i.html [accessed 28 Feb 2012].

Driscoll, C. and Gregg, M. (2010), 'My profile: The ethics of virtual ethnography', *Emotion, Space and Society*, 3(1): 15–20.

Duffy, M.E. (2002), 'Methodological issues in Web-based research', *Journal of Nursing Scholarship*, 34(1): 83–88.

Eagle, N., Pentland, A.S. and Lazer, D. (2009), 'Inferring friendship network structure by using mobile phone data', *Proceedings of the National Academy of Sciences*, 106(36): 15274–78.

Econsultancy (2011), *Internet Statistics Compendium*, Econsultancy.com Ltd.

Ellison, N., Steinfield, C. and Lampe, C. (2006), 'Spatially bounded online social networks and social capital: The role of Facebook', Annual Conference of the International Communication Association, Dresden, Germany, June 19–23.

Ellison, N.B., Steinfield, C. and Lampe, C. (2007), 'The benefits of Facebook "friends": social capital and college students' use of online social network sites', *Journal of Computer-Mediated Communication*, 12(4): 1143–68.

Elmes, D.G., Kantowitz, B.H. and Roediger, H.L. (1999), *Research Methods in Psychology* (6th ed.), Pacific Grove: Brooks/Cole Publishing Company.

Ess, C. (2002), 'Ethical Decision-Making and Internet Research: Recommendations from the AoIR Ethics Working Committee', Association of Internet Researchers Ethics Working Committee. http://www.aoir.org/reports/ethics.pdf [accessed 28 Feb 2012].

Ess, C. (2009), *Digital Media Ethics (Digital Media and Society)*, Cambridge: Polity Press.

ESRC (2010), *Framework for Research Ethics (FRE)*, Swindon: Economic and Social Research Council.

Etherington, K. (2004), *Becoming a Reflexive Researcher: Using Our Selves in Research*, London: Jessica Kingsley.

Eynon, R., Fry, J. and Schroeder, R. (2008), 'The ethics of internet research', in N. Fielding, R.M. Lee and G. Blank (eds.), *The Handbook of Online Research Methods*, Thousand Oaks, CA: Sage Publications.

Eysenbach, G. and Till, J. (2001), 'Ethical issues in qualitative research on internet communities', *British Medical Journal*, 323(7321): 1103–05.

Facer, K. and Sandford, R. (2010), 'The next 25 years? Future scenarios and future directions for education and technology', *Journal of Computer Assisted Learning* 26(1): 74–93.

Fang, J., Shao, P. and Lan, G. (2009), 'Effects of innovativeness and trust on web survey participation', *Computers in Human Behavior*, 25(1): 144–52.

Field, A. and Hole, G J. (2003), *How to Design and Report Experiments*, London: Sage Publications.

Fielding, N. (2010), 'Virtual fieldwork using access grid', *Field Methods*, 22(3): 195–216.

Fielding, N., Lee, R.M. and Blank, G. (eds.) (2008), *The Handbook of Online Research Methods*, Thousand Oaks, CA: Sage Publications.

Fielding, N. and Lee, R.M. (2008), 'Qualitative e-Social Science/Cyber-Research', in N. Fielding, R.M. Lee and G. Blank (eds.), *The Handbook of Online Research Methods*, Thousand Oaks, CA: Sage Publications.

Fields, D. and Kafai, Y. (2009), 'A connective ethnography of peer knowledge sharing and diffusion in a tween virtual world', *International Journal of Computer-Supported Collaborative Learning*, 4(1): 47–68.

Finholt, T. and Sproull, L.S. (1990), 'Electronic groups at work', *Organization Science*, 1(1): 41–64.

Fischer, M., Lyon, S. and Zeitlyn, D. (2008), 'The internet and the future of social science research', in N. Fielding, R.M. Lee and G. Blank (eds.), *The Handbook of Online Research Methods*, Thousand Oaks, CA: Sage Publications.

Fleming, C.M. and Bowden, M. (2009), 'Web-based surveys as an alternative to traditional mail methods', *Journal of Environmental Management*, 90(1): 284–92.

Flick, U. (2009a), *An Introduction to Qualitative Research* (4th ed.), London: Sage Publications.

Flick, U. (2009b), 'Sampling', in U. Flick, *An Introduction to Qualitative Research* (4th ed.), London: Sage Publications.

Fortun, K. (2001), *Advocacy after Bhopal: Environmentalism, Disaster, New Global Orders*, Chicago: University of Chicago Press.

Foster, G. (1994), 'Fishing with the net for research data', *British Journal of Educational Technology*, 25(2): 91–97.

Fowler, F.J. (2008), *Survey Research Methods (Applied Social Research Methods)* (4th ed.), London: Sage Publications.

Fox, F., Morris, M. and Rumsey, N. (2007), 'Doing synchronous online focus groups with young people: methodological reflections', *Qualitative Health Research*, 17(4): 539–47.

Frankel, M. and Siang, S. (1999), *'Ethical and Legal Aspects of Human Subjects Research on the Internet'*, American Association for the Advancement of Science Workshop Report. http://www.aaas.org/spp/sfrl/projects/intres/report.pdf [accessed 28 Feb 2012].

Freeman, L.C. (1984), 'The impact of computer-based communication on the social structure of an emerging social scientific speciality', *Social Networks*, 6: 201–21. http://moreno.ss.uci.edu/39.pdf [accessed 28 Feb 2012].

Frick, A., Bächtiger, M.T., and Reips, U.-D. (2001), 'Financial incentives, personal information, and dropout in online studies', in U.-D. Reips and M. Bosnjak (eds.), *Dimensions of Internet Science*, Lengerich, Germany: Pabst Science, 209–19.

Friedman, D. and Sunder, S. (1994), *Experimental Methods: A Primer for Economists*, Cambridge: Cambridge University Press.

Gaiser, T. (1997), 'Conducting online focus groups: A methodological discussion', *Social Science Computer Review*, 15(2): 135–44.

Gaiser, T.J. (2008), 'Online focus groups', in N. Fielding, R.M. Lee and G. Blank (eds.), *The Handbook of Online Research Methods*, Thousand Oaks, CA: Sage Publications, 290–306.

Gaiser, T.J. and Schreiner, A.E. (2009), *A Guide to Conducting Online Research*. London: Sage Publications.

Galesic, M. and Bosnjak, M. (2009), 'Effects of questionnaire length on participation and indicators of response quality in a web survey', *Public Opinion Quarterly*, 73(2): 349–60.

Ganassali, S. (2008), 'The influence of the design of web survey questionnaires on the quality of responses', *Survey Research Methods*, 2(1): 21–32.

Garcia, A.C., Standlee, A.I., Bechkoff, J. and Cui, Y. (2009), 'Ethnographic approaches to the internet and computer-mediated communication', *Journal of Contemporary Ethnography*, 38(1): 52–84.

Gatson, S.N. and Zweerink, A. (2004), 'Ethnography online: "natives" practising and inscribing community', *Qualitative Research*, 4(2): 179–200.

Gibson, W. (1984), *Neuromancer*, New York: City Lights Books.

Goodwin, J., Dolbear, C. and Hart, G. (2008), 'Geographical linked data: The administrative geography of Great Britain on the semantic web', *Transactions in GIS*, 12: 19–30.

Göritz, A.S. (2006), 'Cash lotteries as incentives in online panels', *Social Science Computer Review*, 24(4): 445–59.

Goritz, A.S. (2007), 'Using online panels in psychological research', in A.N. Joinson, K.Y.A. McKenna, T. Postmes, and U.-D. Reips, (eds.) *Oxford Handbook of Internet Psychology (Oxford Library of Psychology)*, Oxford: Oxford University Press, 473–85.

Gosling, S.D., Vazire, S., Srivastava, S. and John, O.P. (2004), 'Should we trust web-based studies? A comparative analysis of six preconceptions about internet questionnaires', *The American Psychologist*, 59(2): 93–104. http://darkwing.uoregon.edu/~sanjay/pubs/webstudies.pdf [accessed 28 Feb 2012].

Gosling, S., and Johnson, J.A. (eds.) (2010), *Advanced Methods for Conducting Online Behavioral Research*, Washington D.C: American Psychological Association (APA).

Greiner, B., Jacobsen, H.-A. and Schmidt, G. (2002), 'The Virtual Laboratory Infrastructure for Controlled Online Experiments in Economics', Max Planck Institute for Research into Economic Systems, Strategic Interaction Group, Jena. http://www.billingpreis.mpg.de/hbp02/schmidt.pdf [accessed 28 Feb 2012].

Grimes, S.M. (2008), 'Researching the researchers: market researchers, child subjects and the problem of "informed" consent', *International Journal of Internet Research Ethics*, 1(1): 66–91.

Grodzinsky, F.S. and Tavani H.T (2010), 'Applying the "Contextual Integrity" Model of Privacy to Personal Blogs in the Blogospher', *International Journal of Internet Research Ethics*, 3(1): 38–47.

Hafner, K. and Lyon, M. (1996), *Where Wizards Stay Up Late: The Origins Of The Internet*, New York: Simon and Schuster.

Hagel, J.H. and Roth, A.E. (1997), *The Handbook of Experimental Economics*, Princeton, New Jersey: Princeton University Press.

Hagen, P., Robertson, T., Kan, M. and Sadler, K. (2005), 'Emerging research methods for understanding mobile technology use', in *Proceedings of the 17th Australia conference on Computer-Human Interaction: Citizens Online: Considerations for Today and the Future*, OZCHI '05, Narrabundah, Australia: Computer-Human Interaction Special Interest Group (CHISIG) of Australia, 1–10. http://portal.acm.org/citation. cfm?id=1108417 [accessed 28 Feb 2012].

Hamilton, R.J. and Bowers, B.J. (2006), 'Internet recruitment and E-Mail interviews in qualitative studies', *Qualitative Health Research*, 16(6): 821–35.

Hamman, R. (1997), The application of ethnographic methodology in the study of cybersex, *Cybersociology*, 1(1): 1–7. http://collections.lib.uwm. edu/cipr/image/140.pdf [accessed 28 Feb 2012].

Hammersley, M. and Atkinson, P. (2007), *Ethnography: Principles in Practice* (3rd ed), London: Routledge.

Harris, C. (1997), 'Developing online market research methods and tools', paper presented to ESOMAR Worldwide Internet Seminar, Lisbon July 1997.

Harris, P. (2008), *Designing and Reporting Experiments in Psychology* (3rd ed), Buckingham: Open University Press.

Hauben, M. and Hauben, R. (1997), *Netizens: On the History and Impact of Usenet and the Internet*, Los Alamitos, CA: IEEE Computer Society Press.

Healey, B. (2009), *Successful Online Surveys*, http://inquisio.co.nz/ resources/successful-online-surveys-v1.pdf [accessed 28 Feb 2012].

Herring, S.C. and Paolillo, J.C. (2006), 'Gender and genre variation in weblogs', *Journal of Sociolinguistics*, 10(4): 439–59.

Hesse-Biber, S.N., and Leavy, P. (eds) (2008), *Handbook of Emergent Methods*, New York: Guilford Press.

Hewson, C.M., Laurent, D. and Vogel, C.M. (1996), 'Proper methodologies for psychological and sociological studies conducted via the internet', *Behavioral Research Methods, Instruments and Computers*, 28(2): 186–91.

Hewson, C., Yule, P., Laurent, D. and Vogel, C. (2003), *Internet Research Methods*, London: Sage Publications.

Hewson, C., Yule, P., Laurent, D. and Vogel, C. (2002), *Internet Research Methods: A Practical Guide for the Social and Behavioural Sciences (New Technologies for Social Research series)*, London: Sage Publications.

Hinchcliffe, V. and Gavin, H. (2009), 'Social and virtual networks: Evaluating synchronous online interviewing using instant messenger', *The Qualitative Report*, 14(2): 318–40.

Hine, C.M. (2000), *Virtual Ethnography*, London: Sage Publications.

Hine, C.M. (2005), 'Research Sites and Strategies: Introduction', in Hine, C.M., *Virtual Methods: Issues in Social Research on the Internet*, Oxford: Berg Publishers.

Hine, C.M. (ed.) (2005), *Virtual Methods*, Oxford: Berg Publishers.

Hine, C.M. (2008), 'Virtual ethnography: Modes, varieties, affordances', in N. Fielding, R.M. Lee and G. Blank (eds.), *The Handbook of Online Research Methods*, Thousand Oaks, CA: Sage Publications.

Hookway, N. (2008), '"Entering the blogosphere:" some strategies for using blogs in social research', *Qualitative Research*, 8(1): 91–113.

Honing, H. and Reips, U–D. (2008), 'Web-based versus Lab-based Studies: A Response to Kendall', *Empirical Musicology Review*, 3(2): 73–77. http://emcap.iua.upf.edu/showEmcap/publications/Honing-reips-2008.pdf [accessed 28 Feb 2012].

Hooley, T., Hutchinson, J. and Watts, A.G. (2010), *Careering Through The Web. The Potential of Web 2.0 and 3.0 Technologies for Career Development and Career Support Services*, London: UKCES.

Horton, J.J., Rand, D.G. and Zeckhauser, R.J. (2010), *The Online Laboratory: Conducting Experiments in a Real Labor Market*, Cambridge: Harvard University.

Howe, J. (2008), *Crowdsourcing: Why the Power of the Crowd Is Driving the Future of Business*, New York: Crown Business.

Hudson, J.M. and Bruckman, A. (2005), 'Using Empirical Data to Reason about Internet Research Ethics'. http://www.cc.gatech.edu/~asb/papers/hudson-bruckman-ecscw05.pdf [accessed 28 Feb 2012].

Im, E.O., Chee, W., Tsai, H.M., Bender, M. and Lim H.J. (2007), 'Internet communities for recruitment of cancer patients into an internet survey: a discussion paper', *International Journal of Nursing Studies*, 44(7): 1261–69.

International Telecommunication Union (2010), 'Key Global Telecom Indicators for the World Telecommunication Service Sector'. http://www.itu.int/ITU-D/ict/statistics/at_glance/KeyTelecom.html [accessed 28 Feb 2012].

Israel, M. and Hay, I. (2006), *Research Ethics for Social Scientists*, London: Sage Publications.

James, N.R. (2003), 'Teacher Professionalism, Teacher Identity: How Do I See Myself?' Unpublished Doctorate of Education Thesis, University of Leicester, School of Education, July.

James, N. and Busher, H. (2006), 'Credibility, authenticity and voice: dilemmas in online interviewing', *Qualitative Research*, 6(3): 403–20.

James, N. and Busher, H. (2009), *Online Interviewing*, London: Sage Publications.

Johns, M.D., Chen S.-L.S., and Hall, G. J. (eds.) (2004), *Online Social Research: Methods, Issues, and Ethics*, New York: Peter Lang.

Joinson, A.N. (2005), 'Internet Behaviour and the Design of Virtual Methods', in C. Hine, *Virtual Methods: Issues in Social Research on the Internet*, Oxford: Berg, 21–34.

Joinson, A.N. (2001), 'Self-disclosure in computer-mediated communication: The role of self-awareness and visual anonymity', *Eur. J. Soc. Psychol.*, 31(2): 177–92.

Joinson, A.N, McKenna, K.Y.A, Postmes, T. and Reips, U–D. (ed.) (2007), *Oxford Handbook of Internet Psychology* (Oxford Library of Psychology), Oxford: Oxford University Press.

Jones, S. (1995), *Cybersociety: Computer Mediated Communication and Community*, Newbury Park, CA: Sage Publications.

Joy-Gaba, J.A., and Nosek, B.A. (2010), 'The surprisingly limited malleability of implicit racial evaluations', *Social Psychology*, 41(3): 137–46.

Kacmirek, L. (2008), 'Internet Survey Software Tools', in N. Fielding, R.M. Lee and G. Blank (eds.), *The Handbook of Online Research Methods*, Thousand Oaks, CA: Sage Publications.

Kanayama, J. (2003), 'Ethnographic research on the experience of Japanese elderly people online', *New Media and Society*, 5(2): 267–88.

Karchmer, R.A. (2001), 'The journey ahead: Thirteen teachers report how the internet influences literacy and literacy instruction in their K-12 classrooms', *Reading Research Quarterly*, 36(4): 442–66.

Kazmer, M. and Xie, B. (2008), 'Qualitative interviewing in internet studies: Playing with the media, playing with the method', *Information, Communication, and Society*, 11(2): 257–78.

Keen, A. (2007), *The Cult of the Amateur: How the Democratization of the Digital World is Assaulting Our Economy, Our Culture, and Our Values*, New York: Doubleday.

Kehoe, C. and Pitkow, J. (1996), 'Surveying the territory: GVU's five WWW user surveys', *The World Wide Web Journal* [Online], 1(3): 77–84.

Keller, F., Gunasekharan, S., Mayo, N. and Corley, M. (2009), 'Timing accuracy of web experiments: a case-study using the WebExp software package', *Behavior Research Methods*, 41(1): 1–12.

Kelly, K. (2007), 'Predicting the next 5000 days of the web'. TED talk. www. ted.com/index.php/talks/kevin_kelly_on_the_next_5_000_days_of_ the_web.html [accessed 28 Feb 2012].

Kelso, L. and Barchard, K.A. (2005), 'Moving from the lab to the Internet: Getting started', in *Arizona-Nevada Academy of Science Annual Meeting*. http://faculty.unlv.edu/img/img/conference\%20posters/ Advantages\%20and\%20Disadvantages\%20of\%20Online\%20 Research.pdf [accessed 28 Feb 2012].

Kerr, I., Lucock, C. and Steeves, V. (2009), *Lessons from the Identity Trail: Anonymity, Privacy and Identity in a Networked Society*, New York: Oxford University Press.

Kiesler, S. and Sproull, L.S. (1986), 'Response effects in the electronic survey', *Public Opinion Quarterly*, 50(3): 402–13.

King, G. (2011), 'Ensuring the Data-Rich Future of the Social Sciences', *Science* 331(6018): 719–21.

King, S.A. (1996), 'Researching internet communities: Proposed ethical guidelines for reporting of results', *The Information Society*, 12(2): 119–27.

King, N. and Horrocks, C. (2010), *Interviews in Qualitative Research*, London: Sage Publications.

Kivits, J. (2005), 'Online interviewing and the research relationship', in C. Hine (ed.), *Virtual Methods: Issues in Social Research on the Internet*, Oxford: Berg, 35–49.

Knowles, C. and Sweetman, P. (2004), *Picturing the Social Landscape: Visual Methods and the Sociological Imagination*, London: Routledge.

Konstan, J.A. and Chen, Y. (2007), 'Online Field Experiments: Lessons from CommunityLab'. http://www.ncess.ac.uk/events/conference/2007/ papers/paper185.pdf [accessed 28 Feb 2012].

Kozinets, R.V. (2002), 'The field behind the screen: Using the method of Netnography to research Market-Oriented virtual communities', *Journal of Marketing Research*, 39(1): 61–72. http://kozinets. net/__oneclick_uploads/2009/07/field_behind_round3.pdf [accessed 28 Feb 2012].

Kozinets, R.V. (2009), *Netnography: Doing Ethnographic Research Online*, Thousand Oaks, CA: Sage Publications.

Kozinets, R.V. (2010), *Netnography: The Marketer's Secret Weapon. How Social Media Understanding Drives Innovation*, New York: NetBase. http://info.netbase.com/rs/netbase/images/Netnography_WP.pdf [accessed 28 Feb 2012].

Kozlov, M.D. and Johansen, M.K. (2010), 'Real behavior in virtual environments: psychology experiments in a simple virtual-reality paradigm using video games', *Cyberpsychology, behavior and social networking*, 13(6): 711–14.

Krantz, J.H. (1995–2011), *Psychological Research on the Net*. http://psych.hanover.edu/research/exponnet.html [accessed 28 Feb 2012].

Krantz, J.H., Ballard, J. and Scher, J. (1997), 'Comparing the results of laboratory and World-Wide Web samples on the determinants of female attractiveness', *Behavior Research Methods, Instruments, and Computers*, 29(2): 264–69.

Krantz, J.H. and Dalal, R.S. (2000), Validity of web-based psychological research, in M.H. Birnbaum (ed.), *Psychological experiments on the Internet*, San Diego, CA: Academic Press, 35–60.

Kraut, R., Olson, J. Banaji, M., Bruckman, A., Cohen, J. and Couper, M. (2004), 'Psychological research online: report of the Board of Scientific affairs' advisory group on the conduct of research on the internet', *American Psychologist*, 59(2), 105–17.

Krueger, R.A. and Casey, M.A. (2009), *Focus Groups: A Practical Guide for Applied Research* (4th ed.), London: Sage Publications.

Krug, S. (2005), *Don't Make Me Think: A Common Sense Approach to Web Usability* (2nd ed.), Berkeley: New Riders Press.

Krysan, M. and Couper, M.P. (2006), 'Race of Interviewer Effects: What Happens on the Web?' *International Journal of Internet Science*, 1(1): 17–28.

Kvale, S. and Brinkmann, S. (2008), *Interviews: Learning the Craft of Qualitative Research Interviewing* (2nd ed.), London: Sage Publications.

Lamb, M. (1998), 'Cybersex: Research notes on the characteristics of the visitors to online chat rooms', *Deviant Behavior*, 19(2): 121–35.

Lang, K.R. and Hughes, J. (2007), 'Issues in online focus groups: Lessons learned from an empirical study of Peer-to-Peer filesharing system users', *European Journal of Business Research Methods*, 2(2): 95–110.

Langer, R. and Beckman, S.C. (2005), 'Sensitive research topics: netnography revisited', *Qualitative Market Research: An International Journal*, 8(2): 189–203.

Lanier, J. (2010), *You Are Not a Gadget: A Manifesto*, London: Penguin Books.

Larew, C. (2008), 'In response to: Cantrell A.M. and Lupinacci, P. (2007) Methodological issues in online.data collection', *Journal of Advanced Nursing*, 60(5): 544–49.

Leander, K.M. and Mckim, K.K. (2003), 'Tracing the everyday "sitings" of adolescents on the internet: a strategic adaptation of ethnography across online and offline spaces', *Education, Communication and Information*, 3(2): 211–40.

Lee, R.M., Fielding, N. and Blank, J. (2008), 'The internet as a research medium: An editorial introduction to the Sage handbook of online research methods', in N. Fielding, R.M. Lee and G. Blank (eds.), *The Handbook of Online Research Methods*, Thousand Oaks, CA: Sage Publications.

Leiner, B.M., Cerf, V.G., Clark, D.D., Kahn, R.E., Kleinrock, L., Lynch, D.C., Postel, J., Roberts, L.G. and Wolff, S. (2009), 'A brief history of the internet', *ACM SIGCOMM Computer Communication Review*, 39(5): 22–31.

Levitt, S.D. and List, J.A. (2009), 'Field Experiments in Economics: The Past, the Present, and the Future', *European Economic Review*, 53(1), 1–18.

Lewis, M. (2008), 'New strategies of control: Academic freedom and research ethics boards', *Qualitative Inquiry*, 14(5): 684–99.

Lievrouw, L.A. and Carley, K. (1990), 'Changing patterns of communication among scientists in an era of "telescience,"' *Technology in Society*, 12(4): 457–77.

Lipinski, T.A. (2008), 'Emerging Legal Issues in the Collection and Dissemination of Internet-Sourced Research Data: Part I, Basic Tort Law Issues and Negligence', *International Journal of Internet Research Ethics*, 1(1): 92–114.

Liu, Y. (2007), 'A comparative study of learning styles between online and traditional students', *Journal of Educational Computing Research*, 37(1): 41–63.

Lozar M.K., Bosnjak M., Berzelak J., Haas I. and Vehovar V. (2008), 'Web Surveys versus Other Survey Modes: A Meta-Analysis Comparing Response Rates', *International Journal of Market Research*, 50(1): 79–104.

Lüders, C. (2004), 'The Challenges of Qualitative Research', in U. Flick, E. von Kardorff and I. Steinke (eds.), *A Companion to Qualitative Research*, London: Sage Publications, 359–64.

MacDougall, C. and Fudge, E. (2001), 'Planning and recruiting the sample for focus groups and In-Depth interviews', *Qualitative Health Research*, 11(1): 117–26.

Madge, C., Meek, J., Wellens, J. and Hooley, T. (2009), 'Facebook, social integration and informal learning at university: It is more for socialising and talking to friends about work than for actually doing work', *Learning, Media and Technology*, 34(2): 141–55.

Madge, C., O'Connor, H., Wellens, J., Hooley, T. and Shaw, R. (2006), 'Exploring online research methods, incorporating TRI–ORM; an online research methods training programme for the social science community'. http://www.restore.ac.uk/orm/ [accessed 28 Feb 2012].

Madge, C., O'Connor, H., Wellens, J., Hooley, T. and Shaw, R. (2006a), 'Advantages and disadvantages of online interviewing. Exploring online research methods, incorporating TRI–ORM; an online research methods training programme for the social science community'. http://www.restore.ac.uk/orm/interviews/intads.htm [accessed 28 Feb 2012].

Madge, C., O'Connor, H., Wellens, J., Hooley, T. and Shaw, R. (2006b), 'Designing online interviews. Exploring online research methods, incorporating TRI–ORM; an online research methods training programme for the social science community'. http://www.restore. ac.uk/orm/interviews/intdesign.htm [accessed 28 Feb 2012].

Malinowski, B. (1922), *Argonauts of the Western Pacific*, London: Routledge.

Mann, C. and Stewart, F. (2000), *Internet Communication and Qualitative Research: A Handbook for Researching Online*, London: Sage Publications.

Markham, A.N. (2004), 'Internet communication as a tool for qualitative research', in D. Silverman (ed.), *Qualitative Research: Theory, Method and Practice*, London: Sage Publications, 95–125.

Markham, A.N. (2004), 'The internet as research context', in C. Seale, G. Gobo, J.F. Gubrium and D. Silverman (eds.), *Qualitative Research Practice*, London: Sage Publications, 328–44.

Mason, P. (2005), 'Visual data in applied qualitative research: lessons from experience', *Qualitative Research*, 5(3): 325–46.

Maulana, A.E. and Eckhardt, G.M. (2007), 'Just friends, good acquaintances or soul mates? An exploration of web site connectedness', Qualitative Market Research: An International Journal, 10(3): 227–42.

McKee, H.A. and Porter J.E. (2009), The Ethics of Internet Research: a rhetorical case-based process (Digital Formations). New York: Peter Lang, first printing ed.

Meho, L.I. (2006), 'E-Mail interviewing in qualitative research: A Methodological discussion', Journal of the American Society for Information Science and Technology, 57(10): 1084–95.

Merico, D., Gfeller, D. and Bader, G.D. (2009), 'How to visually interpret biological data using networks', Nature Biotechnology, 27(10): 921–24.

Mertens, D.M., and Ginsberg, P.E. (2008), The Handbook of Social Research Ethics, London: Sage Publications.

Meyerson, P. and Tryon, W.W. (2003), 'Validating internet research: a test of the psychometric equivalence of internet and in-person samples', Behavior Research Methods, Instruments, and Computers, 35(4): 614–20.

Mislove, A., Viswanath, B., Gummadi, K.P. and Druschel, P. (2010), 'You are who you know: inferring user profiles in online social networks', in Proceedings of the third ACM international conference on Web search and data mining, WSDM '10, New York: ACM, 251–60.

Morgan Stanley (2010), 'Internet Trends', CM summit 7 June 2010. http://www.slideshare.net/CMSummit/ms-internet-trends060710final [accessed 28 Feb 2012].

Morton, H. (2001), 'Introduction: computer-mediated communication and Australian Anthropology and sociology', Special Issue of Social Analysis, 45(1): 3–11.

Murray, P.J. (1997), 'Using virtual focus groups in qualitative research', Qualitative Health Research, 7(4): 542–54.

Murray, C. and Sixsmith, J. (1998), 'E-mail: A qualitative research medium for interviewing?', International Journal of Social Research Methodology, 1(2): 103–21.

Musch, J. and Reips, U.-D. (2000), 'A brief history of Web experimenting', in M.H. Birnbaum (ed.), Psychological Experiments on the Internet, San Diego: Academic Press, 61–87.

Nag, M. (2010), Mapping Networks: A New Method for Integrating Spatial and Network Data, Princeton: Princeton University.

Nagel, L., Blignaut, S. and Cronjé, J. (2007), 'Methical Jane: Perspectives on an undisclosed virtual student', *Journal of Computer-Mediated Communication*, 12(4), article 10. http://jcmc.indiana.edu/vol12/issue4/nagel.html [accessed 28 Feb 2012].

Nardi, B. and Harris, J. (2006), 'Strangers and friends: collaborative play in world of warcraft'. In *CSCW '06: Proceedings of the 2006 20th anniversary conference on Computer supported cooperative work*, (pp. 149–158). New York, NY, USA: ACM. http://darrouzet-nardi.net/bonnie/pdf/fp199-Nardi.pdf [accessed 28 Feb 2012].

Nardi, B., Ly, S. and Harris, J. (2007), 'Learning Conversations in World of Warcraft', *World*, 1–10. http://www.artifex.org/~bonnie/pdf/Nardi-HICSS.pdf [accessed 28 Feb 2012].

Newman, I. and McNeil, K. (1998), *Conducting Survey Research in the Social Sciences*, Lanham, MD: University Press of America.

Nelson, M. and Otnes, C.C. (2005), 'Exploring cross-cultural ambivalence: a netnography of intercultural wedding message Publications boards', *Journal of Business Research*, 58(1): 89–95.

Nicholson, T., White, J. and Duncan, D. (1998), 'Drugnet: A pilot study of adult recreational drug use via the WWW', *Substance Abuse*, 19(1): 109–21.

Nissenbaum, H. (2004), 'Privacy as contextual integrity', *Washington Law Review*, 79(1): 119–57.

Norman, A.T., and Russell, C.A. (2006), 'The pass-along effect: Investigating word-of-mouth effects on online survey procedures', *Journal of Computer-Mediated Communication*, 11(4): 1085–1103.

O'Connor, D. (2010), 'Apomediation and Ancillary Care: Researchers' Responsibilities in Health-Related Online Communities', *International Journal of Internet Research Ethics*, 3: 87–103.

O'Connor, H. and Madge, C. (2001), 'Cyber-mothers: Online synchronous interviewing using conferencing software', *Sociological Research Online*, 5(4). http://www.socresonline.org.uk/5/4/o'connor.html [accessed 28 Feb 2012].

O'Connor, H. and Madge, C. (2003), 'Focus groups in cyberspace': using the internet for qualitative research, *Qualitative Market Research: An International Journal*, 6(2): 133–43.

O'Connor, H., Madge, C., Shaw, R. and Wellens, J. (2008), 'Internet-based interviewing', in N. Fielding, R.M. Lee and G. Blank (eds.), *The Handbook of Online Research Methods*, Thousand Oaks, CA: Sage Publications.

Odih, P. (2004), 'Using the internet', in Seale, C. (ed.), *Researching Society and Culture* (2nd ed.), London: Sage Publications.

O' Dochartaigh, N. (2001), *The Internet Research Handbook: A Practical Guide for Students and Researchers in the Social Sciences*, London: Sage Publications.

Office for National Statistics (2010), 'Internet Access 2010 Households and Individuals', *Statistical Bulletin*, London: ONS. http://www.ons.gov.uk/ons/rel/rdit2/internet-access---households-and-individuals/2011/stb-internet-access-2011.html [accessed 28 Feb 2012].

O'Lear, S.R.M. (1996), 'Using Electronic Mail (E-mail) Surveys for Geographic Research: Lessons from a survey of Russian environmentalists', *The Professional Geographer* 48(2): 213–22.

Oliver, P. (2010), *The Student's Guide to Research Ethics* (2nd ed), Buckingham: Open University Press.

O'Neil, K.M., Penrod, S.D. and Bornstein, B.H. (2003), 'Web-based research: methodological variables' effects on dropout and sample characteristics', *Behavior Research Methods, Instruments, and Computers*, 35(2): 217–26.

Online Psychology Research UK (2011), *Online Research Resources* http://www.onlinepsychresearch.co.uk/researchers/online-research-resources/ [accessed 28 Feb 2012].

Open University (2006), *Beyond Reasonable Doubt: A Guide to Designing Experiments in the Behavioural Sciences*, Buckingham: Open University Worldwide.

Orgad, S. (2009), 'How can researchers make sense of the issues involved in collecting and interpreting online and offline data?', Annette Markham and Nancy Baym (eds.), *Internet inquiry: conversations about method*, Thousand Oaks, CA: Sage Publications, 33–53. http://eprints.lse.ac.uk/23979/1/How_can_researchers_make_sense_of_the_issues_involved_in_collecting_and_interpreting_online_and_offline_data_%28LSEROI%29.pdf [accessed 28 Feb 2012].

Orgad, S. (2005), 'From online to offline and back: moving from online to offline relationships with research informants', in C. Hine (ed.), *Virtual Methods: Issues in Social Research on the Internet*, Oxford: Berg, 51–65.

Orgad, S. (2005), 'Internet Behaviour and the Design of Virtual Methods', in C. Hine (ed.), *Virtual Methods: Issues in Social Research on the Internet*. Oxford: Berg, 51–65.

O'Hara, K. and Shadbolt, N. (2008), *The Spy in the Coffee Machine: The End of Privacy as we Know it*, Oxford: Oneworld.

Opdenakker, R. (2006), 'Advantages and disadvantages of four interview techniques in qualitative research', *Forum: Qualitative Social Research*, 7(4). http://www.qualitative-research.net/index.php/fqs/article/view/175/391 [accessed 28 Feb 2012].

O'Reilly, T. (2005), 'What is web 2.0: Design patterns and business models for the next generation of software'. http://oreilly.com/web2/archive/what-is-web-20.html [accessed 28 Feb 2012].

O'Riordan (2010), 'Internet research ethics: Revisiting the relations between technologies, spaces, texts and people'. http://eresearch-ethics.org/position/internet-research-ethics-revisiting-the-relations-between-technologies-spaces-texts-and-people/ [accessed 28 Feb 2012].

Oringderff, J. (2004), '"My way": Piloting an online focus group', *International Journal of Qualitative Methods*, 3(3): 1–10. http://www.ualberta.ca/~iiqm/backissues/3_3/pdf/oringderff.pdf [accessed 28 Feb 2012].

Orr, L.L. (1998), *Social Experiments: Evaluating Public Programs With Experimental Methods*, London: Sage Publications.

O'Schaefer, D.R. and Dillman, D.A. (1998), 'Development of standard email methodology', *Public Opinion Quarterly*, 62(3): 378–97.

Paccagnella, L. (1997), 'Getting the seat of your pants dirty: Strategies for ethnographic research on virtual communities', *Journal of Computer Mediated Communication*, 3(1): 267–88.

Pain, R.. and Francis, P. (2003), 'Reflections on participatory research', *Area*, 35(1): 46–54.

Paolacci, G., Chandler, J. and Ipeirotis, P.G. (2010), 'Running experiments on Amazon Mechanical Turk', *Judgment and Decision Making*, 5(5): 411–19.

Parry, O. and Mauthner, N.S. (2004), 'Whose data are they anyway?' *Sociology*, 38(1): 139–52.

Peterson, R.A. (2001), 'On the Use of College Students in Social Science Research: Insights from a Second Order Meta Analysis', *The Journal of Consumer Research*, 28 (3): 450–61.

Platt, J. (1996), *A History of Sociological Research Methods in America 1920–1960*, Cambridge: Cambridge University Press.

Platt, J. (2002), The history of the interview, in J.F. Gubrium and J. A. Holstein (eds), *Handbook of Interview Research: Context and Method.* Thousand Oaks, CA: Sage Publications.

Porter, S.R. and Whitcomb, M.E. (2003), 'The impact of contact type on web-survey response rates', *Public Opinion Quarterly*, 67(4): 579–89.

Procter, R., Williams, R. and Stewart, J. (2010), 'If you build it, will they come? How researchers perceive and use web 2.0', London: Research Information Network. www.rin.ac.uk/system/files/attachments/ web_2.0_screen.pdf [accessed 28 Feb 2012].

Rand, D.G. (2011), 'The promise of Mechanical Turk: How online labor markets can help theorists run behavioral experiments, *Journal of Theoretical Biology*'. http://www.people.fas.harvard.edu/~drand/ rand_jtb_2011.pdf [accessed 28 Feb 2012].

Rathi, D. and Given, L.M. (2010), 'Research 2.0: A framework for qualitative and quantitative research in web 2.0 environments', *Hawaii International Conference on System Sciences*, 5–8 January 2010.

Rea, L. and Parker, R.A. (2005), *Designing and Conducting Survey Research: A Comprehensive Guide (Jossey Bass Public Administration Series)* (3rd ed.), San Francisco, CA: Jossey-Bass.

Read, K.E. (1980), *The High Valley*, New York: Columbia University Press.

Reed-Danahay, D. (1997), *Auto/ethnography: Rewriting the Self and the Social (Explorations in Anthropology)*, Oxford: Berg Publishers.

Reid, E. (1996), 'Informed Consent in the Study of On-Line Communities: A Reflection on the Effects of Computer-Mediated Social Research', *The Information Society*, 12(2): 169–74.

Reingold, H. (1993), *The Virtual Community: Home Steading on the Electronic Frontier*, Reading, MA: Addison-Wesley.

Reips, U.-D. (1995a), 'The web's experimental psychology lab', in J. Musch and U.-D. Reips (2000), *A brief history of web experimenting*, in M.H. Birnbaum (ed.), *Psychological experiments on the Internet*, San Diego, CA: Academic Press, 61–87.

Reips, U.-D. (1995b), 'The web experiment method', in J. Musch and U.-D. Reips (2000), *A brief history of web experimenting*, in M.H. Birnbaum (ed.), *Psychological experiments on the Internet*, San Diego, CA: Academic Press, 61–87.

Reips, U.-D. (1997), 'Das psychologische Experimentieren im Internet (Psychological experimenting on the internet)', in B. Batinic (ed.), *Internet für Psychologen*, Göttingen, Germany: Hogrefe, 245–65.

Reips, U.-D. (1999), 'Online research with children', U.-D. Reips, B. Batinic, W. Bandilla, M. Bosnjak, L. Gräf, K. Moser and A. Werner (eds.), *Current Internet Science – Trends, Techniques, Results* (Aktuelle Online-Forschung – Trends, Techniken, Ergebnisse), Zürich: Online Press.

Reips, U–D (2000), 'The Web Experiment Method: Advantages, disadvantages, and solutions', in M.H. Birnbaum (ed.), *Psychological Experiments on the Internet*, San Diego, CA: Academic Press, 89–118.

Reips, U.-D. (2001), 'The Web Experimental Psychology Lab: Five years of data collection on the internet', *Behavior Research Methods, Instruments, and Computers*, 33(2): 201–11.

Reips, U.-D. (n.d), Tools for internet-based data collection. http://www.iscience.eu/ [accessed 28 Feb 2012].

Reips, U.-D. (2002a), 'Standards for internet-based experimenting', *Experimental Psychology*, 49(4): 243–56.

Reips, U.-D. (2002b), 'Internet–based psychological experimenting: Five dos and five don'ts', *Social Science Computer Review*, 20(3): 241–49.

Reips, U.-D. (2007), 'The methodology of internet-based experiments', in *The Oxford Handbook of Internet Psychology*, Oxford: Oxford University Press.

Richardson, S., and McMullan, M. (2007), 'Research ethics in the UK: What can sociology learn from health?', *Sociology* , 41(6): 1115–32.

Ritchie, J. and Lewis, J. (2003), *'Qualitative Research Practice: A Guide for Social Science Students and Researchers'*, London: Sage Publications.

Reynolds, R. and de Zwart, M. (2010), 'The Duty To "Play": Ethics, EULAs and MMOs', *International Journal of Internet Research Ethics*, 3(1).

Roberts, L.D. and Parks, M.R. (2001), 'The social geography of gender switching in virtual environments on the internet', in E. Green and A. Adam (eds.) *Virtual Gender: Technology, Consumption and Gender*, London: Routledge, 265–85.

Robson, K. (1999), 'Employment experiences of ulcerative colitis and Crohn's disease sufferers.' Unpublished doctoral dissertation, University of Wales, Cardiff, UK.

Rodriguez, A. and Resnick, M.L. (2010), 'Head to head: Remote usability testing takes on live usability testing in the HFES ultimate fighting challenge', *Human Factors and Ergonomics Society Annual Meeting Proceedings*, 759–62.

Rosenberg, A. (2010), 'Virtual world research ethics and the private/public distinction', *International Journal of Internet Research Ethics*, 3(1).

Russell, B. and Purcell, J. (2009), *Online Research Essentials: Designing and Implementing Research Studies*, New York: Wiley.

Ruhleder, K. (2000), The virtual ethnographer: Fieldwork in distributed electronic environments. *Field Methods*, 12(1): 3–17.

Rutter, J. and Smith, G.W.H. (2005), 'Ethnographic presence in nebulous settings', C. Hine (ed.), *Virtual Methods: Issues in Social Science Research on the Internet*, Oxford: Berg.

Ryan, J. (2010), *A History of the Internet and the Digital Future*, London: Reaktion Books Ltd.

Sade-Beck, L. (2004), 'Internet ethnography: Online and offline', *International Journal of Qualitative Methods*, 3(2): 45–51.

Salganik, M.J. and Watts, D.J. (2009), 'Web-Based experiments for the study of collective social dynamics in cultural markets', *Topics in Cognitive Science*, 1(3): 439–68.

Salmons, J. (2009), *Online Interviews in Real Time*, London: Sage Publications.

Sanders, T. (2005), 'Researching the online sex community', in C. Hine (ed), *Virtual Methods: Issues in Social Research*, Oxford: Berg.

Sax, L.J., Gilmartin, S.K. and Bryant, A.N. (2003), 'Assessing response rates and nonresponse bias in web and paper surveys', *Research in Higher Education*, 44(4): 409–32.

Schaefer, D.R. and Dillman, D.A. (1998), 'Development of a Standard E-mail Methodology: Results of an Experiment', *Public Opinion Quarterly*, 62(3): 378–97.

Schmidt, W.C. (1997), 'World-Wide Web survey research: Benefits, potential problems and solutions', *Behavior Research Methods, Instruments, and Computers*, 29(2): 274–79.

Schnoebelen, T. and Kuperman, V. (2009), 'Using Amazon Mechanical Turk for linguistic research: Fast, cheap, easy, and reliable'. http://www.stanford.edu/~tylers/notes/empirical/Schnoebelen-Kuperman-Mechanical_Turk.pdf [accessed 28 Feb 2012].

Schroeder, R. (2007), 'An overview of ethical and social issues in shared virtual environments', *Futures*, 39(6): 704–17.

Schuldt, B.A. and Totten, J.W. (1994), 'Electronic mail vs. mail survey response rates', *Marketing Research*, 6(1): 36–9.

Scott Jones, J. and Watt, S. (2010), *Ethnography in Social Science Practice*, Abingdon, Oxon: Taylor & Francis.

Seale, C. (2004), 'History of Qualitative Methods', in: C. Seale (ed.), *Researching Society and Culture* (2nd ed.), London: Sage Publications.

Sedgwick, M. and Spiers, J. (2009), 'The use of video-conferencing as a medium for the qualitative interview', *International Journal of Qualitative Methods*, 8(1). http://ejournals.library.ualberta.ca/index. php/IJQM/article/view/1826/0 [accessed 28 Feb 2012].

Seko, Y. (2006), Analyzing Online Suicidal Murmurs, *Association of Internet Researchers IR 7.0 – Internet Convergences*, Brisbane. http://aoir. org/conferences/past/ir-7-2006/ [accessed 28 Feb 2012].

Sheehan, K. (2001), 'E-mail Survey Response Rates: A Review', *Journal of Computer- Mediated Communication (JCMC,)* 6(2). http://jcmc.indiana. edu/vol6/issue2/sheehan.html [accessed 28 Feb 2012].

Sheehan, K.B. and McMillan, S.J. (1999), 'Response variation in e-mail surveys: An exploration', *Journal of Advertising Research*, 39(4): 45–54.

Shih, T.-H. and Fan, X. (2008), 'Comparing response rates from web and mail surveys: A Meta-Analysis', *Field Methods*, 20(3): 249–71.

Shin, H.K. and Kim, K.K. (2010), 'Examining identity and organizational citizenship behaviour in computer-mediated communication', *Journal of Information Science*, 36(1): 114–26.

Shirky, C. (2003), 'Power Laws, Weblogs and Inequality'. http://akgul. bilkent.edu.tr/extreme-democracy/Chapter%20Three-Shirky.pdf [accessed 28 Feb 2012]

Shirky, C. (2009), *Here Comes Everybody: The Power of Organizing Without Organizations*, London: Penguin.

Shirky, C. (2010), *Cognitive Surplus: Creativity and Generosity in a Connected Age* (Kindle Edition), London: Penguin.

Shoham, A. (2004), 'Flow experiences and image making: An online chat-room ethnography', *Psychology and Marketing*, 21(10): 855–82.

Sikes, P., and Piper, H. (2010), 'Ethical research, academic freedom and the role of ethics committees and review procedures in educational research', *International Journal of Research and Method in Education*, 3(3): 205–13.

Silver, D. (2000), 'Looking backwards, looking forwards: cyberculture studies 1990–2000', in D. Gauntlett (ed.), *Web Studies. Rewiring Media Studies for the Digital Age*, London: Arnold, 19–30.

Silverman, D. (2009), *Doing Qualitative Research: A Practical Handbook* (3rd ed.), London: Sage Publications.

Slater, D. (1998), 'Trading sexpics on IRC: embodiment and authenticity on the internet', *Body and Society*, 4(4): 91–117.

Slater, M., Antley, A., Davison, A., Swapp, D., Guger, C., Barker, C., Pistrang, N. and Sanchez-Vives, M.V. (2006), 'A virtual reprise of the Stanley Milgram obedience experiments', *PLoS ONE* , 1(1): 1–10.e39+.

Smith, C. (1997), 'Casting the Net: surveying an internet population', *Journal of Computer-Mediated Communication*, 3(1).

Smith, M.A. and Leigh, B. (1997), 'Virtual subjects: using the internet as an alternative source of subjects and research environment', *Behaviour Research Methods, Instruments and Computers*, 29(4): 496–505.

Stanley, L., and Wise, L. (2010), 'The ESRC's 2010 framework for research ethics: Fit for research purpose?', *Sociological Research Online*, 15(4).

Stern, S.R. (2003), 'Encountering distressing information in online research: A consideration of legal and ethical responsibilities', *New Media and Society*, 5(2): 249–66.

Stewart, D.W., Shamdasani, P.N. and Rook, D. (eds) (2007), *Focus Groups: Theory and Practice (Applied Social Research Methods)* (2nd ed), London: Sage Publications.

Stewart, F., Eckermann, E. and Zhou, K. (1998), 'Using the internet in qualitative public health research: A comparison of Chinese and Australian young women's perceptions of tobacco', *Internet Journal of Health Promotion*. http://rhpeo.net/ijhp-articles/1998/12/index.htm [accessed 28 Feb 2012].

Stewart, K. and Williams, M. (2005), 'Researching online population: the use of online focus groups for social research', *Qualitative Research*, 5(4): 395–416.

Stieger, S. and Goritz, A.S. (2006), 'Using instant messaging for internet-based interviews', *Cyberpsychology and Behaviour*, 9(5): 552–59.

Suri, S. and Watts, D.J. (2011), 'Co-operation and contagion in Web-Based, networked public goods experiments', *PLoS ONE* , 6(3): 3–8.

Sweeney. L, (2000), 'Simple Demographics Often Identify People Uniquely', Carnegie Mellon University, Data Privacy Working Paper 3. Pittsburgh.

Swoboda, S.J., Muehlberger, N., Weitkunat, R.. and Schneeweiss, S. (1997), 'Internet surveys by direct mailing: An innovative way of collecting data', *Social Science Computer Review*, 15(3): 242–55.

Symonds, J.E. and Gorard, S. (2010), 'Death of mixed methods? Or the rebirth of research as a craft', *Evaluation and Research in Education*, 23(2): 121–36.

Tapscott, D. and Williams, A.D. (2006), *Wikinomics: How Mass Collaboration Changes Everything*, London: Atlantic Books.

Tashakkori, A. and Teddlie, C. (1998), *Mixed Methodology: Combining Qualitative and Quantitative Approaches*, Thousand Oaks, CA: Sage Publications.

Thelwall, M. (2008), 'Social networks, gender, and friending: An analysis of MySpace member profiles', *Journal of the American Society for Information Science and Technology*, 59(8): 1321–30.

Thelwall, M. (2010), 'Researching the Public Web', E Research Ethics. http://eresearch-ethics.org/position/researching-the-public-web/ [accessed 28 Feb 2012].

Thomas, J. (1996), 'Introduction: A Debate about the Ethics of Fair Practices for Collecting Social Science Data in Cyberspace', *The Information Society*, 12(2): 107– 17.

Thomas, J. (2004), 'Reexamining the ethics of internet research: Facing the challenge of overzealous oversight', in M.D. Johns, S.-L.S. Chen and G.J. Hall (eds.) (2004) *Online Social Research: Methods, Issues, and Ethics*, New York: Peter Lang, 187–201.

Toma, C. and Hancock, J. (2009), 'Catching liars: The linguistic signature of deception in online profiles', paper presented at the annual meeting of the NCA 95th Annual Convention, Chicago Hilton and Towers, Chicago, IL, Nov 11, 2009. http://www.allacademic.com/meta/p367023_index.html [accessed 28 Feb 2012].

Tonkiss, F. (2004), 'History of social statistics and the social survey', in C. Seale (ed.), *Researching Society and Culture* (2nd ed.), London: Sage Publications.

Turkle, S. (1999), 'Cyberspace and identity', *Contemporary Sociology*, 28(6): 643–48.

Turkle, S. (1995), *Life on the Screen: Identity in the Age of the Internet*, New York: Touchstone.

Turney, L. and Pocknee, C. (2005), 'Virtual Focus Groups: New Frontiers in Research', *The International Journal of Qualitative Methods*, 4(2): 32–43.

Valkenburg, P.M. and Peter, J. (2008), 'Adolescents' identity experiments on the Internet', *Communication Research* , 35(2): 208–31.

Van Laerhoven, K. (2011), 'ISWC 2010: The latest in wearable computing research', *IEEE Pervasive Computing*, 10(1): 8–10.

Varnhagen, C.K., Gushta, M., Daniels, J., Peters, T.C., Parmar, N., Law, D., Hirsch, R., Takach, B.S.S. and Johnson, T. (2005), 'How informed is online informed consent?' *Ethics and behavior*, 15(1): 37–48.

Vavoula, G. and Sharples, M. (2009), 'Meeting the challenges in evaluating mobile learning: A 3-level evaluation framework', *International Journal of Mobile and Blended Learning*, 1(2): 54–75.

Vidich, A.J. and Lyman, S.M. (1994), 'Qualitative methods: Their history in sociology and social anthropology', in N.K. Denzin and Y.S. Lincoln, *Handbook of Qualitative Research*. Thousand Oaks, CA: Sage Publications.

Voida, A., Mynatt, E.D., Erickson, T. and Kellogg, W.A. (2004), 'Interviewing over instant messaging', in *CHI '04 Extended abstracts on Human factors in computing systems*, New York: ACM, 1344–47.

Walstrom, M.K. (2004), 'Ethics and engagement in communication scholarship: Analyzing public, online support groups as researcher/participant-experiencer', in E.A. Buchanan (ed), *Virtual research ethics: Issues and controversies*, Hershey, PA: Information Science Publishing, 174–202.

Walther, J.B. (2002), 'Research Ethics in Internet-Enabled Research: Human Subjects Issues and Methodological Myopia', Ethics and Information Technology, 4(3): 205–16.

Ward, K.J. (1999), The cyber-ethnographic (re)construction of two feminist online communities, *Sociological Research Online*, 4(1). http://www.socresonline.org.uk/4/1/ward.html [accessed 28 Feb 2012].

Webster, M. and Sell, J. (2007), *Laboratory Experiments in the Social Sciences*, San Diego: Academic Press.

Weigend, A. (1994), 'Music recognition experiments', in J. Musch and U.-D. Reips (2000), A brief history of web experimenting, in M.H. Birnbaum (ed.), *Psychological experiments on the Internet*. San Diego, CA: Academic Press, 61–87.

Weinberger, D. (2003), *Small Pieces Loosely Joined: A Unified Theory of the Web*, Cambridge MA: Perseus Books Group.

Weinberger, D. (2008), *Everything Is Miscellaneous: The Power of the New Digital Disorder*, New York: Henry Holt.

Welch, N. and Krantz, J. (1996), 'The World-Wide Web as a medium for psychoacoustical demonstrations and experiments: Experience and results', *Behavior Research Methods, Instruments, and Computers*, 28(2): 192–96.

Wesch, M. (2008), 'An anthropological introduction to YouTube'. http://www.youtube.com/watch?v=TPAO-lZ4_hU [accessed 28 Feb 2012].

Whiteman, N. (2010), 'Control and Contingency: Maintaining Ethical Stances in Research', *International Journal of Internet Research Ethics*, 3(1): 6–22.

Whitty, M.T. (2004), 'Peering into online bedroom windows: considering the ethical implications of investigating internet relationships and sexuality', in E. Buchanan (ed.), *Readings in Virtual Research Ethics: Issues and Controversies*, Hershey, USA: Idea Group Inc., 2004, 203–18.

Williams, M. (2003), *Making Sense of Social Research*, London: Sage Publications.

Wiersma, W. (n.d.), From web–forms to virtual worlds: Opportunities and Challenges posed by Four Types of Online Experiment. http://wybowiersma.net/pub/essays/Wiersma,Wybo,From_web-forms_to_virtual_worlds.pdf [accessed 28 Feb 2012].

Wiles, R., Pain, H. and Crow, G. (2010), *Innovation in Qualitative Research Methods: A Narrative Review*. Southampton: ESRC National Centre for Research Methods, School of Social Sciences, University of Southampton.

Williams, M. (2007), 'Avatar watching: participant observation in graphical online environments', *Qualitative Research*, 7(1): 5–24.

Williamson, H. (2004), *The Milltown Boys Revisited*, Oxford: Berg Publishers.

Wood, A., Stankovic, J., Virone, G., Selavo, L., He, Z., Cao, Q., Doan, T., Wu, Y., Fang, L. and Stoleru, R. (2008), 'Context-aware wireless sensor networks for assisted living and residential monitoring', *IEEE Network*, 22(4), 26–33.

Wright, K.B. (2005), 'Researching internet-based populations: Advantages and disadvantages of online survey research, online questionnaire authoring software packages, and web survey services', *Journal of Computer-Mediated Communication*, 10 (3). http://jcmc.indiana.edu/vol10/issue3/wright.html [accessed 28 Feb 2012].

W3C (2010), 'Accessibility', part of *Web Design and Applications*. http://www.w3.org/standards/webdesign/accessibility [accessed 28 Feb 2012].

W3C (1999), 'Resource Description Framework (RDF) Model and Syntax Specification'. http://www.w3.org/TR/PR-rdf-syntax/ [accessed 28 Feb 2012].

Xenos, M. and Bennett, W.L. (2007), 'The disconnection in online politics: the youth political web sphere and US election sites, 2002–2004', *Information, Communication and Society*, 10(4): 443–64.

Yan, T., Conrad, F.G., Tourangeau, R. and Couper, M.P. (2010), 'Should I stay or should I go: The effects of progress feedback, promised task duration, and length of questionnaire on completing web surveys', *International Journal of Public Opinion Research*, 23(2): 131–47.

Zelditch, M. (1969), 'Can you really study an army in the laboratory?' in A. Etzioni and E.N. Lehman (eds.), *A sociological reader on complex organization*, New York: Holt, Rinehart, and Winston, 528–39.

Zittrain, J. (2009), *The Future of the Internet: And How to Stop It*, London: Penguin Books.

Zudilova-Seinstra, E., Adriaansen, T. and Liere, R. (2009), 'Overview of interactive visualization', in *Trends in Interactive Visualization*, London, Springer-Verlag, 1–13.

Index